Lean Six Sigma: Cost Reduction Strategies

By Ade Asefeso MCIPS MBA

Second Edition

ISBN-13: 978-1499775075

ISBN-10: 1499775075

Publisher: AA Global Sourcing Ltd
Website: http://www.aaglobalsourcing.com

Table of Contents

Disclaimer 7

Dedication 8

Section 1: Lean Six Sigma 9

Chapter 1: Introduction 11

Chapter 2: The History of Six Sigma 15

Chapter 3: History of the Six Sigma Black Belt
Naming Convention 19

Chapter 4: Remembering Bill Smith, Father of Six
Sigma 25

Chapter 5: Six Sigma is not a "Get Rich Quick"
Methodology 33

Chapter 6: Quality Guru's Life Had a Humble
Beginning 39

Chapter 7: Should you Calculate your Process
Sigma? 43

Chapter 8: A Method for Aligning the Six Sigma
Performance Metric 49

Chapter 9: The Champion's Role in Successful Six
Sigma Deployments 53

Chapter 10: The Extended Six Sigma Champion . 57

Chapter 11: Six Critical Success Factors for a Six
Sigma Deployment 63

Chapter 12: You Can't Manage What you Can't
Measure 67

Chapter 13: Driving Six Sigma Success without
Top-level Support 79

Chapter 14: Eight Lessons for Success in Lean Six Sigma Deployment.................85

Chapter 15: Is Process Management Right for your Business? 91

Chapter 16: Successful Six Sigma Deployment.....97

Chapter 17: Aligning Six Sigma with Objectives and Strategies.................107

Chapter 18: Tips for Doing a Deployment Review 111

Chapter 19: 5 Six Sigma Deployment Mistakes and How to Avoid Them.................117

Chapter 20: Six Sigma Unique Features.............123

Chapter 21: Quality Management Tools and Methods Used in Six Sigma.................127

Chapter 22: Six Sigma Implementation Roles.....129

Chapter 23: Criticism of Six Sigma 133

Chapter 24: Design for Six Sigma (DFSS)...........139

Section 2: Overview of Lean Principles.............145

Chapter 25: Lean and Toyota Production System (TPS).................147

Chapter 26: A Brief History of Waste Reduction Thinking.................153

Chapter 27: Design for Manufacture (DFM)......157

Chapter 28: Types of Waste.................161

Chapter 29: Lean Implementation Develops from TPS.................165

Chapter 30: Continuous Improvement.................171

Chapter 31: Is Lean Differences from TPS?.......173

Chapter 32: Lean Goals and Strategy 177

4

Chapter 33: Conclusion 181

Disclaimer

This publication is designed to provide competent and reliable information regarding the subject matter covered. However, it is sold with the understanding that the author and publisher are not engaged in rendering professional advice. The authors and publishers specifically disclaim any liability that is incurred from the use or application of contents of this book.

If you purchased this book without a cover you should be aware that this book may have been stolen property and reported as "unsold and destroyed" to the publisher. In this case neither the author nor the publisher has received any payment for this "stripped book."

Dedication

This book is dedicated to the hundreds of thousands of incredible souls in the world who have weathered through the up and down of recent recession.

To my family and friends who seems to have been sent here to teach me something about who I am supposed to be. They have nurtured me, challenged me, and even opposed me.... But at every juncture has taught me!

This book is dedicated to my lovely boys, Thomas, Michael and Karl. Teaching them to manage their finance will give them the lives they deserve. They have taught me more about life, presence, and energy management than anything I have done in my life.

Section 1: Lean Six Sigma

Chapter 1: Introduction

What does is Lean Six Sigma?

Lean Six Sigma is a synergised managerial concept of Lean and Six Sigma that results in the elimination of the seven kinds of wastes/muda (classified as Defects, Overproduction, Transportation, Waiting, Inventory, Motion and over Processing) and provision of goods and service at a rate of 3.4 defects per million opportunities (DPMO).

Six Sigma seeks to improve the quality of process outputs by identifying and removing the causes of defects (errors) and minimizing variability in manufacturing and business processes. It uses a set of quality management methods, including statistical methods, and creates a special infrastructure of people within the organization ("Black Belts", "Green Belts", etc.) who are experts in these methods. Each Six Sigma project carried out within an organization follows a defined sequence of steps and has quantified financial targets (cost reduction and/or profit increase).

The term Six Sigma originated from terminology associated with manufacturing, specifically terms associated with statistical modelling of manufacturing processes. The maturity of a manufacturing process can be described by a sigma rating indicating its yield, or the percentage of defect-free products it creates. A six sigma process is one in which 99.99966% of the products manufactured are statistically expected to be free of defects (3.4 defects per million). Motorola set a goal of "six sigma" for all of its manufacturing operations, and this goal became a byword for the management and engineering practices used to achieve it.

Lean Six Sigma utilises the DMAIC phases similar to that of Six Sigma. The Lean Six Sigma projects comprise the Lean's waste elimination projects and the Six Sigma projects based on the critical to quality characteristics. The DMAIC toolkit of Lean Six Sigma comprises all the Lean and Six Sigma tools. The training for Lean Six Sigma is provided through the belt based training system similar to that of Six Sigma. The belt personnel are designated as Green Belts, Black Belts and Master Black Belts.

Lean Six Sigma at many organizations simply means a measure of quality that strives for near perfection. But the statistical implications of a Lean Six Sigma program go well beyond the qualitative eradication of customer-perceptible defects. It's a methodology that is well rooted in mathematics and statistics.

The objective of Lean Six Sigma Quality is to reduce process output variation so that on a long term basis, which is the customer's aggregate experience with our process over time, this will result in no more than 3.4 defect Parts per Million (PPM) opportunities (or 3.4 Defects Per Million Opportunities – DPMO). For a process with only one specification limit (Upper or Lower), this results in six process standard deviations between the mean of the process and the customer's specification limit (hence, 6 Sigma). For a process with two specification limits (Upper and Lower), this translates to slightly more than six process standard deviations between the mean and each specification limit such that the total defect rate corresponds to equivalent of six process standard deviations.

Many processes are prone to being influenced by special and/or assignable causes that impact the overall performance of the process relative to the customer's specification. That is, the overall performance of our process as the customer views it might be 3.4 DPMO (corresponding to Long Term performance of 4.5 Sigma). However, our process could indeed be capable of producing a near perfect output (Short Term capability, also known as process entitlement of 6 Sigma).

The difference between the "best" a process can be, measured by Short Term process capability, and the customer's aggregate experience (Long Term capability) is known as Shift depicted as Zshift or sshift. For a "typical" process, the value of shift is 1.5; therefore, when one hears about "6 Sigma," inherent in that statement is that the short term capability of the process is 6, the long term capability is 4.5 (3.4 DPMO – what the customer sees) with an assumed shift of 1.5. Typically, when reference is given using DPMO, it denotes the Long Term capability of the process, which is the customer's experience. The role of the Six Sigma professional is to quantify the process performance (Short Term and Long Term capability) and based on the true process entitlement and process shift; establish the right strategy to reach the established performance objective

As the process sigma value increases from zero to six, the variation of the process around the mean value decreases. With a high enough value of process sigma, the process approaches zero variation and is known as 'zero defects.'

Statistical Take Away

Decrease your process variation (remember variance is the square of your process standard deviation) in order to increase your process sigma. The end result is greater customer satisfaction and lower costs.

Chapter 2: The History of Six Sigma

Six Sigma has evolved over time. The concepts behind Six Sigma can be traced through the centuries as the method took shape into what it is today.

The roots of Six Sigma as a measurement standard can be traced back to Carl Frederick Gauss (1777-1855) who introduced the concept of the normal curve. Six Sigma as a measurement standard in product variation can be traced back to the 1920's when Walter Shewhart showed that three sigma from the mean is the point where a process requires correction. Many measurement standards (Cpk, Zero Defects, etc.) later came on the scene but credit for coining the term "Six Sigma" goes to a Motorola engineer named Bill Smith. (Incidentally, "Six Sigma" is a federally registered trademark of Motorola).

Six Sigma originated as a set of practices designed to improve manufacturing processes and eliminate defects, but its application was subsequently extended to other types of business processes as well. In Six Sigma, a defect is defined as any process output that does not meet customer specifications, or that could lead to creating an output that does not meet customer specifications.[3]

The core of Six Sigma was "born" at Motorola in the 1970s out of senior executive Art Sundry's criticism of Motorola's bad quality. As a result of this criticism, the company discovered a connection between increases in quality and decreases in costs of production. At that time, the prevailing view was that quality costs extra money. In fact, it reduced total costs by driving down the costs for repair or control. Bill Smith subsequently formulated the particulars of the methodology at Motorola in 1986. Six Sigma was heavily inspired by the quality improvement methodologies of the six preceding decades, such as quality control, Total Quality Management (TQM), and Zero Defects, based on the work of pioneers such as Shewhart, Deming, Juran, Crosby, Ishikawa, Taguchi, and others.

In the early and mid-1980s with Chairman Bob Galvin at the helm, Motorola engineers decided that the traditional quality levels measuring defects in thousands of opportunities didn't provide enough granularities. Instead, they wanted to measure the defects per million opportunities. Motorola developed this new standard and created the methodology and needed cultural change associated with it. Six Sigma helped Motorola realize powerful bottom-line results in their organization in fact; they documented more than $16 Billion in savings as a result of our Six Sigma efforts.

Since then, hundreds of companies around the world have adopted Six Sigma as a way of doing business. This is a direct result of many of America's leaders openly praising the benefits of Six Sigma. Leaders such as Larry Bossidy of Allied Signal (now Honeywell), and Jack Welch of General Electric Company. Rumor has it that Larry and Jack were playing golf one day and Jack bet Larry that he could implement Six Sigma faster and with greater results at GE than Larry did at Allied Signal. The results speak for themselves.

Six Sigma has evolved over time. It's more than just a quality system like TQM or ISO. It's a way of doing business. As Geoff Tennant describes in his book Six Sigma: SPC and TQM in Manufacturing and Services: "Six Sigma is many things, and it would perhaps be easier to list all the things that Six Sigma quality is not. Six Sigma can be seen as a vision; a philosophy; a symbol; a metric; a goal; a methodology." I couldn't agree more.

Chapter 3: History of the Six Sigma Black Belt Naming Convention

Not surprisingly, the term Black Belt has its roots in the exotic realm of martial arts. Like a person skilled in the Oriental sport of karate, the Six Sigma Black Belt is self-assured and knowledgeable, the result of intensive training and real-world experience.

Motorola, the company that holds the Six Sigma trademark, says the data-driven defect-reduction process has saved the company more than $16 billion over the past 15 years. Six Sigma has generated similarly stunning results at companies here and abroad in the manufacturing, transactional, and service sectors. All businesses regardless of sector, size, or project link their success to one factor. In Six Sigma manner of speaking, it's the Black Belt.

The term Black Belt refers to project leaders, skilled in the use of statistical methods and interpersonal communication, and dedicated to using Six Sigma methods to ensure customer satisfaction. Green Belts require less training than Black Belts and take responsibility for leading fewer projects, while Master Black Belts spend nearly all of their time consulting, mentoring, and training Green Belts and Black Belts.

Not surprisingly, the term Black Belt has its roots in the exotic realm of martial arts. Like a person skilled in the Oriental sport of karate, the Six Sigma Black Belt is self-assured and knowledgeable, the result of intensive training and real-world experience. The Six Sigma Black Belt is disciplined, purposeful, and decisive, able to lead highly focused efforts aimed at improving a company's bottom line. And, to ensure continued improvement, the Black Belt works affirmatively to identify and mentor new Black Belts.

The evocative term is not without its detractors, however. For some, martial arts is synonymous with violence, attack mode, and bravado, all of which run counter to the term's intended meaning: a methodically executed self-defence. Some companies have changed the names of their process improvement change leaders to move away from these images. Raytheon, for example, has replaced the words Black Belt with Expert, as in Six Sigma Expert and Six Sigma Master Expert. Mount Carmel Health System refers to Black Belts as Guides, and Master Black Belts as Master Guides. Countrywide Financial Corporation has left the Six Sigma and Belt terminology completely behind; instead, they refer to Master Black Belts, Black Belts and Green Belts as Gold, Silver, and Bronze certification levels, respectively. The Vanguard Group has even gone as far as to call their process improvement efforts "Unmatchable Excellence," although much is based on the Six Sigma methodology.

While the late Bill Smith, a Motorola senior engineer and scientist, commonly gets credit for initiating the Six Sigma concept, the wordsmith who originated the belt argot is Dr. Mikel Harry. In 1986-1987 Harry, on authorized sabbatical from Motorola, spent three months at the Unisys Salt Lake Printed Circuit

Facility, where he worked as a technical consultant with Unisys facility manager Clifford Ames. Harry's mission was to solve a costly circuit board production problem.

According to Harry, once the problem was solved, Ames asked him to train others at Unisys. Harry referred to those he trained as process characterization experts, the term he had previously used for trainees at the Motorola Government Electronics Group. Harry remembers brainstorming with Ames to come up with something a little catchier. When Harry suggested Black Belts, Ames responded enthusiastically: "That's sexy! I can sell that." And the rest, as they say, is history.

Because a team approach is the norm among Motorola scientists and engineers, the belt-naming convention may appear to some to have occurred over time and osmotically among Motorola executives. However, Harry cites contracts, reports, and other artifacts that document the terminology's introduction and implementation. The belt terminology, first articulated in a 1988 contract between Unisys and Harry, appears that same year in strategy papers from the first Unisys Black Belt trainees. Harry says he formally introduced the terminology to Motorola in a 1989 white paper, A Strategic Vision for accelerating the implementation of Six Sigma at Motorola, a paper he prepared for then CEO Robert Galvin.

By the early 1990s, the Black Belt nomenclature was hot. Recently retired Quality Director John Lupienski complements Harry's version of the origins of Black Belt terminology in a time line Lupienski prepared for a 1990s Motorola Six Sigma presentation. Lupienski, who participated in Motorola's first Quality Council meetings with Bill Smith and Jack Germain (Motorola's first Vice President of Quality), says the Black Belt program began in 1990 with the organization of a DOE symposium committee. Additional Motorola employees who were present at this time verify these facts.

The following year, Harry established Motorola's Six Sigma Research Institute, which he had proposed in his 1989 Strategic Vision white paper, and served as its founding Director and a senior member of the technical staff. The Institute, a research and testing site, offered a reasonable alternative to the factory floor for simulations and statistical problem solving. As the Institute's Director, Harry relied on the Black Belt framework to move Six Sigma methodology across the corporation.

Harry successfully nurtured the Black Belt model, encouraging other companies to implement it in 1992. Harry says he persuaded those other companies like Texas Instruments, IBM, Kodak, Digital Equipment, and Asea Brown Boveri to share expertise and work with Motorola and the Institute to craft a mutually beneficial training program.

David Hallowell, the Digital representative at that time, recalls the common Black Belt curriculum that the consortium identified, developed and piloted. The statistical part of the body of knowledge was easy to see, but a key insight was the inclusion of a healthy measure of soft skills to deal with the change management, business awareness, and team dynamics critical to real Six Sigma success. The Six Sigma Technical Institute was soon deploying that training for Black Belt candidates. By the end of 1992, the first half-dozen Six Sigma Black Belts had gained recognition in Asia and the United States.

The Black Belt jargon has stuck. In fact, an online Google search for Six Sigma generates a whopping 565,000 keyword matches, many of them about Black Belt training. Just as Six Sigma has outlived early scepticism about its long-term survival, the Green Belt/Black Belt/Master Black Belt designations have emerged as generally accepted business terminology.

Chapter 4: Remembering Bill Smith, Father of Six Sigma

Bill Smith, the Father of Six Sigma, introduced the statistical approach while working at Motorola, where it garnered the company financial benefits and numerous awards.

Bill Smith spent years convincing higher-ups that he really had invented a better mousetrap. Then he spent the rest of his life spreading the word to business professionals, government leaders and educators.

Smith's mousetrap? It was Six Sigma, the TQM spin off that has generated billions of dollars for Motorola, the company where Smith introduced his statistical approach aimed at increasing profitability by reducing defects. Smith, who earned the appellation, Father of Six Sigma, would probably be tickled to know Six Sigma has become so mainstream that it even appears periodically in the widely syndicated comic strip, Dilbert.

As a Motorola employee, Smith did not share directly in the profits generated by the company's Six Sigma applications. However, over the years, he and Motorola garnered numerous awards and recognition for his vital work to improve profitability in America's manufacturing sector. He was especially proud of his role in Motorola's winning the prestigious Malcolm Baldrige National Quality Award. The Baldrige Award came in 1988, two years after Motorola implemented Smith's Six Sigma principles.

Smith's death, only five years later, caught everyone by surprise. He died of a heart attack at work.

Daughter Marjorie Hook, now 37 and president of Clarksville Consulting Group in Austin, Texas, developed an affinity for Six Sigma and occasionally collaborated with her father for a few years after college. Hook said winning the Baldrige Award stands out as a career high point in her father's life.

"He was thrilled that a good thing was happening to Motorola and that Six Sigma had made such a difference," she said. "He drafted Six Sigma long before [Motorola Executive Committee Chairman] Bob Galvin ever took it on board. So, for him, it was the culmination of so many years of work and trying to change the way people think about things. He finally had some phenomenal success at Motorola and he was getting great recognition for it."

Baldrige Award winners agree to share their quality programs with anyone who is interested. Hook said that since Motorola was the first company to win, others were eager to learn more about Six Sigma. "That's one of the primary reasons Six Sigma became so widely known," she said.

"He got to spend the last few years of his life travelling around, teaching and introducing Six Sigma to people," Hook said. "He was so appreciated wherever he went and people were really interested in it. When others started using Six Sigma and seeing results just like Motorola had, he was thrilled."

Not surprisingly, the man behind the methodology was a passionate visionary and a great communicator. Bill Smith was also a perfectionist. Even at home.

"But not in an annoying way," Hook said. "He just did everything the right way because that was the way to do it.

"I think that was just a natural part of his character," she said. "It came through when he was repairing a watch or helping us with a science project or fixing a car or learning to play a musical instrument; he was incredibly talented. He knew how to do absolutely everything."

Hook said he always approached projects methodically and drafted a plan, either on paper or in his mind. "He planned things out, making sure we had the skills and the tools, doing it, and then following through with the cleaning up," Hook said. "Everything had to be done in a complete way. Nothing was ever done sort of off-hand. The standard was always so high."

Bill Smith also made the most of leisure time. He and his wife, Betty, shared a love of music, especially when they were the musicians, she on the piano and he on the organ at their Barrington, Illinois home. However, she suspects he bought her a new baby grand piano to keep her occupied while he devoted spare time to working out statistical programs on his computer.

"One time when he was home in the evening, he had an idea of trading stock options," Betty Smith recalled. "So he would do it on paper and then on the computer for awhile to see how it would work. And it worked very well. Imagine that!"

Bill Smith also used his computer to develop a program that would help him predict winning racehorses. Betty Smith said he programmed a calculator with data about the horses racing at Arlington International Racecourse in Arlington Heights, Illinois. "By golly, I think we won eight of the first nine, and people were following us around," she said.

The Smiths soon joined half a dozen others in a horse-owning partnership, embarking on a lifelong hobby. "We had six horses when he died," Betty Smith said. "They were ours, not part of a partnership. In the beginning, it was lucrative. I think one horse won most of the money. After Bill died, I got rid of all the horses except one. Her grandfather was Seattle Slew, the famous 1977 Triple Crown winner."

Born in Brooklyn, New York, in 1929, Bill Smith graduated from the U.S. Naval Academy in 1952 and studied at the University of Minnesota School of Business. In 1987, after working for nearly 35 years in engineering and quality assurance, he joined Motorola, serving as vice president and senior quality assurance manager for the Land Mobile Products Sector.

In honour of Smith's talents and dedication, Northwestern University's Kellogg Graduate School of Management established an endowed scholarship in Smith's name. Dean Donald P. Jacobs of the Kellogg School notified Motorola's Robert Galvin of the school's intention less than a month after Smith died. "Bill was an extremely effective and inspiring communicator," Jacobs wrote in his July 27, 1993, letter. "He never failed to impress his audience by the depth of his knowledge, the extent of his personal commitment, and the level of his intellectual powers." The school created the scholarship fund in recognition of Smith's "contributions to Kellogg and his dedication to the teaching and practice of quality."

It was a fitting tribute to a man who influenced business students and corporate leaders worldwide with his innovative Six Sigma strategy.

As the one who followed most closely in his footsteps, Marjorie Hook is well-positioned to speculate about Bill Smith's take on the 2003 version of Six Sigma. "Today I think people sometimes try to make Six Sigma seem complicated and overly technical," she said. "His approach was, 'If you want to improve something, involve the people who are doing the job.' He always wanted to make it simple so people would use it."

And would he approve of Six Sigma's evolution? "He'd be thrilled," Hook said.

Many people say that it takes money to make money. In the world of Six Sigma quality, the saying also holds true: it takes money to save money using the Six Sigma quality methodology. You can't expect to significantly reduce costs and increase sales using Six Sigma without investing in training, organizational infrastructure and culture evolution.

Sure you can reduce costs and increase sales in a localized area of a business using the Six Sigma quality methodology and you can probably do it inexpensively by hiring an ex-Motorola or GE Black Belt. I like to think of that scenario as a "get rich quick" application of Six Sigma. But is it going to last when a manager is promoted to a different area or leaves the company? Probably not. If you want to produce a culture shift within your organization, a shift that causes every employee to think about how their actions impact the customer and to communicate within the business using a consistent language, it's going to require a resource commitment. It takes money to save money!

How much financial commitment does Six Sigma require and what magnitude of financial benefit can you expect to receive? We all have people that we must answer to and rhetoric doesn't pay the bills or keep the stockholders happy (anymore). I was tired of reading web pages or hearing people say:

"Companies of all types and sizes are in the midst of a quality revolution. GE saved $12 billion over five years and added $1 to its earnings per share. Honeywell (AlliedSignal) recorded more than $800 million in savings."

"GE produces annual benefits of over $2.5 billion across the organization from Six Sigma."

"Motorola reduced manufacturing costs by $1.4 billion from 1987-1994."

"Six Sigma reportedly saved Motorola $15 billion over the last 11 years."

The above quotations may in fact be true, but pulling the numbers out of the context of the organization's revenues does nothing to help a company figure out if Six Sigma is right for them. For example, how much can a $10 million or $100 million company expect to save?

I investigated what the companies themselves had to say about their Six Sigma costs and savings. I didn't believe anything that was written on third party websites, was estimated by "experts," or was written in books on the topic. I reviewed literature and only captured facts found in annual reports, website pages and presentations found on company websites.

While recent corporate events like the Enron and WorldCom scandals might lead us to believe that not everything we read in a company's annual report is valid, I am going to provide the following information based on the assumption that these Six Sigma companies operate with integrity until proven otherwise.

I investigated Motorola, Allied Signal, GE and Honeywell. I choose these four companies because they are the companies that invented and refined Six Sigma; they are the most mature in their deployments and culture changes. As the Motorola website says, they invented it in 1986. Allied Signal deployed Six Sigma in 1994, GE in 1995. Honeywell was included because Allied Signal merged with Honeywell in 1999 (they launched their own initiative in 1998). Many companies have deployed Six Sigma between the years of GE and Honeywell I Will leave those companies for another Chapter in this book.

Chapter 5: Six Sigma is not a "Get Rich Quick" Methodology

Six Sigma is not a "get rich quick" methodology. I like to think of it like my retirement savings plan. Six Sigma is a get rich slow methodology the take-away point being that you will get rich if you plan properly and execute consistently.

As GE's 1996 annual report states, "It has been estimated that less than Six Sigma quality, i.e., the three-to-four Sigma levels that are average for most U.S. companies, can cost a company as much as 10-15 percent of its revenues. For GE, that would mean $8-12 billion." With GE's 2001 revenue of $111.6 billion, this would translate into $11.2-16.7 billion of savings. Although $2 billion worth of savings in 1999 is impressive, it appears that even GE hasn't been able to yet capture the losses due to poor quality or maybe they're above the three-to-four Sigma levels that are the average for most U.S. companies?

In either case, 1.2-4.5 percent of revenue is significant and should catch the eye of any CEO or CFO. For a $30 million a year company, that can translate into between $360,000 and $1,350,000 in bottom-line-impacting savings per year. It takes money to make money. Is investing in Six Sigma quality, your employees and your organization's culture worth the money? Only you and your executive leadership team can decide the answer to that question.

The man whose ideas led to corporations adopting Six Sigma and other quality management strategies warns that U.S and UK. companies are moving too slowly in improving the quality of business procedures, products and services. These nations position in the world economy is at risk, according to Dr. Joseph M. Juran.

Juran, dean of quality professionals worldwide, told an audience which had come to Stamford, Connecticut (USA) to mark his 100th year and the Juran Institute's 25th anniversary: "The U.S. improvement of quality has been evolutionary, not revolutionary. We have exported jobs and lost entire industries. If these standards continue, there will be a severe risk that the U.S. will lose its status as an economic superpower."

Pressing the issue of quality as he has for decades, Juran made his remarks at a luncheon in his honour. Family, friends and numerous business executives who have benefited from his advice celebrated his 100th birthday, which actually comes on Dec. 24. They also recognized the institute he established in 1979 to address quality management issues. The institute is located in Wilton, Connecticut (USA).

Chief executives should personally become leaders of their companies' quality control efforts, Juran said. He credited Motorola for starting its own quality control university in the 1980s and blazing the trail in the Six Sigma management strategy.

Juran's Role in Japanese Leadership in Quality

Japanese industrialists established quality measures as a business priority in the 1950s and 1960s. Leaders among those Japanese industrialists have given great credit to Juran for advice he first gave them in 1954 during a presentation he made in Japan. Although Juran was the one who delivered the message, along with another American management icon, W. Edwards Deming, it is the Japanese who deserve the credit for incorporating the ideas into their manufacturing and quality control processes, Juran said.

"They knew they needed help. They listened, and they translated my books into Japanese. I gave lectures like that in a lot of countries, but they took it a lot further," Juran said. The result was a nation that incorporated quality management into nearly every facet of business, distancing Japan from the rest of the world, he said.

"The United States is not the world leader in quality. The leader is Japan. Before World War II it was the exporter of shoddy goods," Juran told the audience. "They tried to gain power through trade. Their executives knew they had to improve their quality. The rest is history."

Juran's message about quality management resonated among top executives at those Japanese businesses, according to Noriaku Kano, engineering professor in the Department of Industrial Management and Engineering at Tokyo University of Science. Kano, a well-known name in quality management himself, travelled from Tokyo for the Juran celebration.

"It was important to the development of Japan," said Kano, who was a graduate student in Japan when he first met Juran in 1966. In fact, Juran developed such a reputation among Japanese industrialists that he was decorated by the emperor, said Kano, one of a series of speakers who had stories to tell about their dealings with Juran and his institute, which specializes in working with corporations and non-profits on quality management issues.

Quality Leaders Worldwide Praise Juran's Contributions

Curt Reimann, former director of the Malcolm Baldridge National Quality Award and retired director for quality programs at the National Institute of Standards and Technology, recalled Juran's testimony before Congress about Japan's emphasis on quality as its way to compete in the world economy. "I think there was a great deal of hand wringing, but there needed to be action," Reimann said. Hence the Baldridge competition was started in 1986, with the assistance of Juran as a member of the award's board of overseers.

A. Blanton Godfrey, a former chief executive officer of the Juran Institute and dean of the School of Textiles at North Carolina State University, contended that U.S. companies made a crucial error by not adopting Juran's philosophies in the 1950s when the Japanese saw the benefits. "It was productivity in the 1950s and not quality. The objective wasn't making it good. It was making it fast," Godfrey said. "The Japanese listened and became exporters."

"I had no idea in 1924 that the subject of managing for quality would, during my lifetime, expand in importance, become a growth industry, and undergo a wrenching world revolution. Yet it did." - Dr. Joseph M. Juran

One of Juran's pupils, Enrique Maso, travelled to the celebration from Barcelona, Spain, to thank Juran for his tutelage. Maso recalled a day in 1949 when he spent five hours in Washington Square in New York City, discussing business management with Juran, who at the time was an instructor at New York University. "I owe everything to Professor Juran," said Maso, who became a major player in several Spanish industries and served as the mayor of Barcelona.

Lennart Sandholm of Sweden-based Sandholm Associates told the audience that he already was familiar with Juran's strategies when he met Juran in 1965 while a quality control manager at Electrolux in Sweden. He tried to attend Juran's seminars whenever one was being held in Sweden. In all, Juran made 31 visits to Sweden. "The visits that you made laid a foundation for a long friendship," Sandholm told Juran, adding that he has been an inspiration to Swedish companies. "You are the person outside of my family that has had the greatest influence on my life," Sandholm said.

David Hutchins, a principal in David Hutchins International Limited, came to the celebration from the United Kingdom. He recalled that Juran was speaking to him and others in London the day Indira Ghandi was assassinated in October 1984. Even though a noisy crowd assembled in the street outside the building, Juran kept his commitment, speaking over the tumult.

Juran's ideas have been adopted by many major corporations in the U.S., Japan, Spain, Sweden, the United Kingdom and Canada, according to Joseph DeFeo, the current president and CEO of the Juran Institute. DeFeo met Juran in 1985 when he was a manager at Perkin Elmer. "The values he taught us saved that company for about 20 years," said DeFeo, who helped organize the fete for Juran. Under DeFeo's leadership, the institute carries on Juran's legacy by helping organizations around the world improve their business management techniques.

Chapter 6: Quality Guru's Life Had a Humble Beginning

What do I have in common with Juran? Is humble beginning!

Juran, who now lives in Rye, New York (USA) with Sadie, his wife of 77 years, immigrated to Minneapolis, Minnesota (USA), before World War I with his mother and five siblings from a small town in the former Austro-Hungarian Empire. His father had preceded the family to the United States three years earlier.

A display outside the meeting room provided guests with an in-depth look at Juran's life, including a copy of his birth certificate, photographs of the Romanian village where he was born and the modest house where he lived with his family in Minnesota. A portrait taken at the time of Juran's graduation from East High School in Minneapolis in 1917 revealed a handsome young man with an eager look, ready to contribute to his adopted homeland.

Like many of that era, Juran worked at a variety of jobs, including labourer, shoe salesman, bootblack, grocery clerk and bookkeeper. But unlike most of his peers, he decided to seek a college degree and in 1920 enrolled at the University of Minnesota. He graduated with a degree in electrical engineering and later earned a law degree. Years later, he showed his appreciation to the university by funding what became the Juran

Centre for Quality Improvement. The university has established a fellowship in his honour, focused on promoting quality in business.

Juran's career has included a stint as head of industrial engineering at Western Electric in the late 1930s, serving as a lend-lease assistant administrator during World War II and later his dedication to consulting on quality management. In 1937, with his conceptualization of the Pareto Principle, Juran became a source for those in business management.

Juran's Quality Handbook, which he wrote in 1951, is now in its fifth printing. His book, Managerial Breakthrough, first published in 1964, presented a more general theory of quality management, which evolved into Six Sigma — a quality management process adopted by Motorola, General Electric and now many other corporations. Many of the 200 celebrants at the luncheon carried Juran's most recent book, Architect of Quality, his autobiography which was published by McGraw-Hill last year.

Juran continues to write about issues and fundamentals in managing for quality, and is planning another book.

After he established the Juran Institute at age 74, one of the first projects was development of a video series on quality improvement that was distributed to companies around the world. "Probably a million people listened to those tapes," Juran said. He finally relinquished the role of leading the institute in 1987, allowing him time to continue lecturing.

Juran Comes from a Family of Achievers

Speaking concisely in a clear tone that belied his age, Juran informed the luncheon audience that he comes from a family of achievers. He introduced his son, Charles, who made a career in agricultural real estate; his daughter, Sylvia, who earned a doctorate in Russian literature; and a cadre of grand children and great-grandchildren who are involved in a variety of professions or are in college.

For Charles Juran, 73, the day was one of celebration and one of memories. "I was brought up to believe in the American dream," he said. "I saw it materialize in our family." He noted that his Uncle Nathan became an Oscar-winning film director, his Aunt Minerva earned a doctoral degree and had a career in education, and his Uncle Rudy founded a municipal bond company. "All of that talent out of that little shack," he mused.

"It was a hard life for my father as a child. There was little difference between the poverty in Minneapolis and in Romania. This is not a personal story of achievement," he said. "It's an American story."

Chapter 7: Should you Calculate your Process Sigma?

Practitioners must learn when and how to calculate the sigma level of a process.

Many people hear about the Six Sigma quality methodology and immediately want to calculate their own process sigma to determine how close (or far) they are from six sigma. My immediate response to them is twofold:
1. Are you currently measuring your process capability?
2. Are you satisfied with your performance?

If the answer to both is yes, then calculating your process sigma may be interesting but not necessary.

When Process Sigma is Not Necessary

Let me illustrate with an example. A power company measures their performance in uptime of available power to their grid. Every minute of potential uptime (power is available) is an opportunity, every minute of downtime (power is not available) is a defect in the eyes of a customer. Data is continuously taken, the process capability is measured, and the yield is calculated to be 99.9%. The power company is satisfied with their current performance (but always looking to improve), and the customer's needs (as collected via Voice of the Customer) are being met.

If the entire company communicates in yield and everyone within the company understands this language, is determining the process sigma level useful? I submit that if the company is pursuing full implementation of the Six Sigma quality methodology across the organization then calculating sigma is appropriate because processes within the organization and between plants can be compared. When a company is only considering Six Sigma for one functional area (power transmission OR bill collection OR call centre) then the company might be better suited to maintain the metrics that everyone currently uses and understands.

How can an organization communicate if everyone doesn't learn the language?

I know what you're thinking, 'Ok Ade, get on with it. I want to calculate my process sigma anyway. How can I do it?' Here is your two minute instruction on calculating your process sigma.

How to Calculate Process Sigma

Consider the power company example from the previous page: A power company measures their performance in uptime of available power to their grid. Here is the 5 step process to calculate your process sigma.

Step 1: Define your Opportunities
An opportunity is the lowest defect noticeable by a customer. This definition, of course, is debatable within the Six Sigma community. Here's a useful

snippet from fellow professionals discussing this point:

"Typically, most products (and services) have more than one opportunity of going wrong. For example, it is estimated than in electronics assembly a diode could have the following opportunities for error: 1) Wrong diode and 2) wrong polarity (inserted backwards), so for each assembly shipped, at least two defect opportunities could be assigned for each diode. Apparently, some manufacturers of large complex equipment with many components prefer to count two opportunities in this case. My point is that this approach dilutes Six Sigma metrics." -Anonymous

Many Six Sigma professionals support the counter point. I always like to think back to the pioneer of Six Sigma, Motorola. They built pagers that did not require testing prior to shipment to the customer. Their process sigma was around six, meaning that only approximately 3.4 pagers out of a million shipped did not function properly when the customer received it. The customer doesn't care if the diode is backwards or is missing, just that the pager works.

Returning to our power company example, an opportunity was defined as a minute of uptime. That was the lowest (shortest) time period that was noticeable by a customer.

Step 2: Define your Defects
Defining what a defect is to your customer is not easy either. You need to first communicate with your customer through focus groups, surveys, or other

voice of the customer tools. To Motorola pager customers, a defect was defined as a pager that did not function properly.

Returning to our power company example, a defect is defined by the customer as one minute of no power. An additional defect would be noticed for every minute that elapsed where the customer didn't have power available.

Step 3: Measure your Opportunities and Defects

Now that you have clear definitions of what an opportunity and defect are, you can measure them. The power company example is relatively straight forward, but sometimes you may need to set up a formal data collection plan and organize the process of data collection. Be sure to read 'Building a Sound Data Collection Plan' to ensure that you gather reliable and statistically valid data.

Returning to our power company example, here is the data we collected:

    a.   Opportunities (last year): 525,600 minutes

    b.   Defects (last year): 500 minutes

Step 4: Calculate your Yield

The process yield is calculated by subtracting the total number of defects from the total number of opportunities, dividing by the total number of opportunities, and finally multiplying the result by 100.

Returning to our power company example, the yield would be calculated as: ((525,600 − 500) / 525,600) * 100 = 99.90%.

Alternatively, the yield can be calculated for you by using the iSixSigma Process Sigma Calculator – just input your process opportunities and defects.

Step 5: Look Up Process Sigma
The final step (if not using the iSixSigma Process Sigma Calculator) is to look up your sigma on a sigma conversion table, using your process yield calculated in

Step 4: Assumptions
No analysis would be complete without properly noting the assumptions that you have made. In the above analysis, we have assumed that the standard sigma shift of 1.5 is appropriate (the calculator allows you to specify another value), the data is normally distributed, and the process is stable. In addition, the calculations are made with using one-tail values of the normal distribution.

Chapter 8: A Method for Aligning the Six Sigma Performance Metric

Some Six Sigma practitioners are concerned about the current method used to calculate Z-scores and express process capability. A proposed modification, based on Berryman's scorecard, may fill the need for a more intuitive and business savvy metric.

The common terminology for describing the capability of a business process is process sigma, or Z-score. Z-scores provide a universal standard performance metric for vastly different processes. According to this standard, a process sigma of 6.0 equates to 3.4 defects per million opportunities (DPMO). This value is obtained by accounting for the fact that any process in control continues to allow for a drift of about 1.5 sigma. The traditional calculation method results in the following Z-scores for error free processes

0 percent error-free yield = negative infinity Z-score
50 percent error-free yield = 1.5 Z-score
99.99966 percent error-free yield = 6.0 Z-score
100 percent error-free yield = positive infinity Z-score

Some Six Sigma practitioners have raised concerns about the current calculation method and the need to develop a more intuitive Z-score. Because a 50 percent error-free yield does not equal a Z-score of zero, the range of Z-scores from negative infinity to positive infinity gives a false sense of symmetry. The asymmetry is due to the belief that any long-term process variability changes by about 1.5 sigma from its short-term variation.

In addition to the asymmetry in the measurement system, there are questions about the appropriateness of using a negative sigma value. While the method and logic used for negative Z-scores is clear, the intuitive meaning of them is not. What does the negative sigma value mean? What is the meaning of a Z-score of zero? As a manager, how should you react to improvements and reward sigma value gains? While the mathematically minded will argue that it is simply a definition, the fact that questions are raised about its appropriateness puts forth a challenge to the Six Sigma community to develop a metric that makes engineering as well as business sense.

The Need for Change

Recently, a Six Sigma team presented their results for a project where the initial process yield was very low, resulting in a low sigma value. A small effort by the project team, however, made a significant change in the sigma score. The management team was excited about the project team's work. But their excitement was not as high for another project where the team was charged with making an improvement within an already high-performing process. The current Z-score calculation method does not provide a clear reflection of the effort required to improve processes at various levels of initial sigma value.

This begs the questions.

1. Should practitioners use a metric that is more intuitive in understanding the initial and subsequent change in sigma value?
2. Should the metric account for the relative effort required to achieve the improvement?

Chapter 9: The Champion's Role in Successful Six Sigma Deployments

Champions have a much larger role in deploying Six Sigma or any other initiative than just removing roadblocks. Champions must be integrated into the business; select projects accurately, adjust the speed of the deployment as necessary, and take responsibility for implementation.

For a Six Sigma deployment to produce the expected results, organizational roles and responsibilities must be clearly defined and aligned. If Executives and Champions are trained and Black Belts and Green Belts aren't, the probability of success decreases to virtually nothing. The reverse is true as well. None of these situations will produce the type of results that will occur when Six Sigma practitioners are placed in the correct support environment.

The Six Sigma Support Structure

The core structure at an operational level is Black Belts supported by Master Black Belts. The Black Belts are trained in the basic problem-solving strategy and methodology. When Black Belts have demonstrated a proclivity for solving difficult projects, are self-starters, are self-reliant to a reasonable extent and put in the time commensurate with the task, they are considered for additional training as Master Black Belts. There is no universally accepted standard for the Master Black Belt curriculum. Additional training is intended to broaden, not necessarily raise the level of, the tool sets that are at the disposal of Master Black Belts. The strategy is to provide Master Black Belts with a wider array of skill sets so they can assist in projects that may become stalled.

Six Sigma Green Belts are critical to the process because they are the key to creating a culture shift. If the shift is attempted by training huge numbers of Black Belts, Black Belts will spend most of their time tripping over each other as they scramble to create the "number of projects" or "dollars saved" metrics imposed by management to motivate them.

A popular theory is that in a change process, one-third is on the fence, one-third is holding back, and one-third is jumping at the new opportunity. These numbers will fluctuate based on the company culture. A conservative company culture will create more fence sitters and resistors. A dynamic company culture will increase the number of people jumping at the new opportunity. Before you can comprehend what the number actually is, you must understand the company culture. Green Belts, in the long run, are the ones who shift the culture.

The relationship between Master Black Belts, Black Belts and Green Belts is well understood due to the intuitive nature of the titles. Getting just this much of the structure bolsters the success model. So what is the rest of the structure?

In most organizations they are referred to as Champions. If you ask people what a Champion does, they will quickly reply, "they remove roadblocks." Superficially, that is true. Champions should remove roadblocks. Champions need to be in a position to defuse any issues that may arise between a Black Belt and another person in the organization, particularly if the issue is with someone with a higher formal position in the company. The Champion should be the buffer that keeps a Black Belt out of a head-to-head confrontation with Managers, Vice Presidents and Directors in the company, allowing Black Belts the freedom to focus on the problem, not engage in some inane territorial dispute. This is the most fundamental function of the Champion.

Chapter 10: The Extended Six Sigma Champion

One critical characteristic for successful Six Sigma Champions is that they are some hybrid of Henry Kissinger and Xena, the Warrior Princess. It may actually be easier to find the mutant offspring of these two leaders than it is to find the complete Champion. Being the complete Champion requires more than diplomatic and warrior skill sets.

Champions must be proficient in four other areas:
1. Business and operations interface
2. Project selection
3. Pace mediation
4. Results implementation

Business and Operations Interface

Champions should know the business they are in and at least be familiar with the technology used in the process. Black Belts are the process/project subject matter experts. Champions must constantly guard against intruding into the process and offering solutions. One of the Champion's primary roles is to assure that operational level projects are aligned with the strategic level business objectives. Project reviews should be conducted not as a tool to manage Black Belts but to assure that the project is progressing as planned and that the result will produce a result that resembles (and aligns with) the needs of the organization. It can also be an opportunity for

Champions to identify other potential areas of improvement.

Many companies have invoked the Balanced Score Card to assure this alignment. It is a good tool to apply metrics to Champions. It can be used as a measurement tool to quantify the performance of Champions in this role.

Six Sigma Project Selection

The basic task of assigning Six Sigma projects remains an enigma for some reason. This is the most fundamental skill of a manager with direct reports. When placed under the microscope of matching a project to a Black Belt, however, Champions will "stand frozen in the headlights." You have to wonder if it is truly such a difficult task or if it is the public nature of their decision that causes them so much consternation. We have seen Black Belts in report-out situations where some top-level manager will remark, "Who picked that project?" This goes back to the Dr. Deming's eighth point: "Drive out fear." This seemingly innocuous remark will infuse fear deep into Champions' hearts. Instead of viewing project selection as an opportunity to improve a part of the process, they perceive it as a potentially career-limiting opportunity. The management staff attending reviews should be coached by either their Six Sigma providers (consultants) or a person with a background in Organizational Development (OD) on how to interact with the people involved in the report-out.

Again, alignment is the key. If the organization truly understands and practices alignment, project selection becomes less of a threat. Furthermore, if the alignment is augmented with process data it is an even easier task. The threatening question is defused to become a discussion of the alignment methods or the data that was used. The personal implications become a non-issue.

Pace Mediation

At the onset of a Six Sigma deployment one or more people are selected to generate a deployment plan. This seems to come from one of two sources; the Six Sigma provider or the internal sponsor. There is an inherent issue with allowing a Six Sigma provider to formulate the plan; cost. If your Six Sigma provider is most concerned with enhancing their own financial position, you could be in trouble. If your Six Sigma provider is more concerned with creating a successful deployment and letting reputation provide the incremental business, you should be fine. In either situation it does not make much sense to abdicate complete control of company resources to a person with limited scope of your business operations.

One should also realize the risks associated with choosing an internal sponsor. The resulting plan will be a direct function of the sponsor's level of Six Sigma knowledge. Many organizations have taken to hiring an Internal Master Black Belt to lead the organizational charge. The risk here is the same as previously mentioned: if the total deployment experience is one deployment, they still have a limited scope. It is the basic calculation for a confidence interval using attribute data and a sample size of one. It is better than zero but probably not a significant difference. The optimum Six Sigma deployment plan is derived from a combination of an internal expert (Business, Six Sigma and Change) and the Six Sigma provider.

Once a plan has been generated and sold at the C-Level it is difficult to modify. Internal people will rarely adjust the plan. Very few deployments are initiated with metrics that quantify the program's results and lead to a decision to accelerate or slow the program. Slowing a Six Sigma initiative too much may cause it to die, no sense of urgency will deprioritize any initiative regardless of which initiative it is. The real issue comes from a person or persons so committed to driving a plan that they see only completion as the success metric. Frequently these programs are quantified in terms of numbers of people trained. This will turn the focus from a results-driven program to a training program.

When a plan is constructed it should have goals, specific targets that will increase customer success/satisfaction, competitive position, technology, etc. These should have metrics. Meeting or not meeting metrics should be analyzed, and adjustments should be made to the program.

Results Implementation

We have labelled Black Belts as Change Agents. Change agents inherit the responsibility for implementing projects with identified potential savings. In many cases the Black Belt project will be cross-functional, and cutting across departmental lines can be hazardous waters to navigate, not to mention the complete lack of formal authority that the Black Belt possesses in these situations. Green Belt projects may be less prone to this ailment, but it may affect them as well.

When a project is completed it should have a calculated potential savings. The finance department of the organization, not the Six Sigma provider, should sign off on this number. The savings should not only have a financial measurement but should also be time bounded. That number represents a reduction in wasted resources for the organization. It is a metric that the Champion should be held accountable for. If a project identifies a $50,000 savings over the next 12 months and it produces only $25,000 because the Champion took six months to get involved in the implementation, then the metric should reflect the lack of involvement. If the plan was executed perfectly and the financial projection was inaccurate, a metric should be in place to reflect that inaccuracy. Just as with anything else, the metrics will drive the performance. If you want accurate projections and timely implementations, you had better place a metric on them.

One of the biggest questions associated with Six Sigma project savings is "are they real." A decision to credit soft savings opens the door to exaggerations. The audit functions in place in companies today should be of a wide enough scope to assure the accuracy of these numbers whether they are from a Six Sigma deployment or any other program that uses cost savings as a metric. The audit function does not necessarily lie within the accounting or finance departments. The process of calculating savings may be well defined, documented and incorporated into some type of Quality System (Business System) audit. Some of the larger companies have internal auditors who have been given responsibility for the accuracy of these numbers as well.

Champions have a much larger role in deploying Six Sigma or any other initiative than just removing roadblocks. The job requires more than just this single task. Champions must be integrated into the business; select projects accurately, adjust the speed of the deployment as necessary, and take responsibility for implementation.

Unless metrics are placed on all responsibilities of a Champion, the organization is placing the deployment at risk. Failure to execute these tasks at even a minimal level can and does propagate turnover of the people your organization spent valuable resources training.

Chapter 11: Six Critical Success Factors for a Six Sigma Deployment

Six Sigma is a powerful tool for solving business problems and driving excellence in organizations. Its benefits can include breakthrough improvements, cost savings, defect reduction, greater customer satisfaction, and higher productivity and efficiency. To reap these benefits, however, organizations must pay close attention to six key factors that can make or break a Six Sigma deployment.

Senior Management Involvement

Top management team members must show their support for the deployment. Simply sending emails is not enough; they must take the responsibility of leading from the front, through involvement in the following areas:

1. Selecting projects and teams
2. Reviewing project milestones
3. Approving improvement ideas
4. Resolving conflicts
5. Recognizing teams

For example, if an organization's chief operating officer (COO) oversees support functions, such as HR, administration, training and finance, etc., the COO, as the sponsor, needs to be involved in projects from selection to closure.

Another important role for the top management is to resolve conflicts between Green Belts, Black Belts or process owners who are working on Six Sigma projects. Because of the power of their position, senior management team members should step in to diffuse situations.

Selection of Six Sigma Projects

When selecting a project, organizations need to make sure that the project has a manageable scope. If the perspective is too wide, the project will demand too many resources and take a long time to complete. As the project drags on, team members may lose interest mid-way through, thus reducing the chances of the project's survival. By selecting projects with manageable scope, the organization will be able to demonstrate early wins, and the Six Sigma program will gain momentum and appreciation.

Another important factor that must be considered while selecting a Six Sigma project is the operational stability of the process. Consider this scenario: A team starts a project to reduce recruitment cycle time. The current process is influenced by the people doing the recruitment. However, the management team has decided to roll out a highly automated recruitment process within the next couple of months. Because of the drastic changes involved, it is easy to imagine that the project will be scrapped mid-way.

Selection of Project Teams

Many organizations find success by selecting a project leader who belongs to the operational process being improved and has a stake in that process. For example, appointing a member of the HR team to lead a project to bring improvements to a finance process simply because the HR team member is available can easily backfire. Sometimes it is worth appointing a co-project lead as a back-up. This is especially helpful if the project is focused on a process or function where the roles and responsibilities of team members change dynamically due to their customers' needs.

Inclusion of Six Sigma Projects in Performance Appraisals

Another significant success factor is the inclusion of project efforts in the performance objectives of all team members working on a project. The objectives should be measurable and have clear deadlines. Communicating these objectives to all the team members and their managers at the beginning of the project will bring accountability and apply positive pressure on the team to deliver as planned.

Customization of Six Sigma to the Organization's Culture

Sometimes organizations use help from an external consultant in deploying Six Sigma. Others may designate a leader from within the organization to act as Champion of the deployment. It is extremely important for an organization to make sure that the consultant or internal Champion understands the purpose of the deployment, as well as the context and culture of the organization.

The consultants or internal Champions must not dump all of their knowledge onto the team members at once. Training needs to be flexible according to the participants' work schedules and carefully designed and delivered, with relevant examples and exercises that suit the business context.

Six Sigma training and mentoring should consist of more than mere academic modules on statistics. The objective should be to transform people into knowledge assets in the areas of root-cause analysis, innovative problem solving and process improvements so that they can bring value to the organization.

Recognition and Celebration

Finally, the management team needs to make sure that there is timely recognition of the effort put in by the project teams and that they are rewarded as per the organization's policies and strategy. The celebration and evangelization of "wins" in a Six Sigma project can generate interest and inspire people to contribute to the organization's journey of excellence.

Remember that the benefits of Six Sigma can include breakthrough improvements, cost savings, defect reduction and greater customer satisfaction.

Chapter 12: You Can't Manage What you Can't Measure

This axiom, while intuitive for most managers and business professionals, is often not applied to the Six Sigma management process itself. For Six Sigma or any other management initiative to yield the advertised results, many factors must be considered, aligned, measured and acted upon. Having been involved with Six Sigma as a consultant to a dozens of companies, I have been in a position to experience a variety of cultures and management systems and their linkage to quantitative results. While there are tremendous differences in management styles and priorities from company to company, one thing is clear. The organizations that focused on continuously measuring and driving management behaviours, including aligning initiatives and priorities, yield a much higher return on their programs than those who leave it to chance.

Consider the cost savings most often discussed in the annual reports of the best Six Sigma companies. They are usually discussing savings in a range of 2 – 3% of sales per year. At 3% of sales this adds as much as 10% per year to operating margin. Motorola reported, through their Six Sigma briefings, that savings for a 10-year period from 1985 to 1995 were $11 billion. GE in 1999 reported $2 billion in savings attributable to Six Sigma, and in their 2001 annual report discussed the completion of over 6,000 Six Sigma projects probably yielding over $3 billion in savings by conservative estimates.

Other organizations that have adopted Six Sigma have experienced far lesser amounts of financial success and organizational "buy in". Many have Six Sigma savings in the range of 0.5% to 1.0% of sales (far less than the benchmarks mentioned above). There have even been cases where entire Six Sigma programs have been scrapped after significant investment due to low returns. How is this possible? Review of these failures and shortfalls has generally concluded that the lack of attention to the Critical Success Factors, for a sustained period of time, created a management vacuum around the program. Thus, the reactive culture that Six Sigma normally ferrets out through attention to data driven analysis returned and overcame the Six Sigma initiative. It's human nature to revert to the old way (the comfortable way) of doing things when under stress.

The positive results don't come easy and are driven by many factors besides management alignment. Without the statistics, the Black Belts, the projects, and the training, none of these results can be realized. But equally, the lack of alignment between people, strategy, customers and processes can quickly derail the best-intentioned initiative and quickly divert the attention of management.

Critical Success Factors and Focus

During most Six Sigma Executive and Champion training events some discussion of Critical Success

Factors takes place. These discussions vary greatly in depth of coverage but usually include a variety of content on.

1. Executive Engagement
2. Management Involvement
3. Communications
4. Resources
5. Projects
6. Discipline and Consequences.

Each one of these Critical Success Factors may be broken down into sub-factors to further define the actions, measurements, roles, responsibilities and behaviours that each slice of the organization must demonstrate to assure success and get significant results.

Let's examine a few Critical Success Factors and their associated sub-factors a little more closely and for clarification.

Critical Success Factor – Executive Engagement

1. Visible, consistent support and an active role in communication and reward.
2. Assuring linkage of Six Sigma to corporate strategies.
3. Clear prioritization (relative to other initiatives, programs and priorities).
4. Requiring the use of facts and data to support actions at all levels of decision-making.
5. Creating accountabilities, expectations, roles and responsibilities for the organization.
6. Conducting and attending regular reviews to assure and verify progress.

Critical Success Factor – Communications
1. Creation and communication of a Human Resources plan to support Six Sigma roles.
2. Regular written communications on Six Sigma news and successes.
3. Development and dissemination of communication aids to management.
4. Advocating and creating a "common language" based on Six Sigma.
5. Communicating pertinent facts about Six Sigma in every company meeting.

Critical Success Factor – Projects
1. Establish a documented 1-year Six Sigma project inventory (and refresh regularly).
2. Assure linkage of Six Sigma projects to critical business and customer needs.
3. Establish projects of appropriate scope and size (significant savings & achievable).
4. Assign a Champion and Black Belt to each project (and hold them accountable).
5. Implement a project tracking system to facilitate replication and reuse.

The documentation of these Critical Success Factors and their sub-factors is merely a first step in the process of assuring their implementation and making them a permanent part of a company's culture and operating system. There is also the issue of assuring their effectiveness and use by the appropriate members of the target organization. Traditional methods of monitoring management behaviours have been largely subjective. There are systems that use Scorecards with red, yellow and green indicators. Still others that simply use check lists. It has occurred to many of us involved in Six Sigma that a better and more quantitative method for measuring, aligning and closing gaps in management performance and behaviour are needed. Especially considering that Six Sigma requires fact and data based decision making and performance enhancement.

The Power of Alignment

A good friend introduced me to the concept of Organizational Alignment several years ago. In his book, The Power of Alignment (John Wiley & Sons, 1998), he presents a compelling case for the need for Organizational Alignment and highlights 30 years of research connecting alignment to success.

The basis of his alignment concept is to collect a large sample of data from the various layers of an organization based around a series of factors and sub-factors. The data is objective in that instead of asking people how they "think they are doing with their own work," you ask employees and management how the organization is doing with its work around a set of specific statements. That data is referenced to a quantitative scale (0-7 for example) and the sub-factors are defined in such a way that the responses may be "drilled," demographically sorted, summarized and analyzed.

When this data is statistically analyzed and displayed many strengths, weaknesses and gaps can be visually displayed. Because George was a fighter pilot for the United States Air Force he likes to look at things from the perspective of a "target." Applying this to management alignment, his preferred display was one that plotted a "numerical gap analysis" on a radar type of chart. The closer that the scores are toward the middle of the target, the tighter the alignment and the higher the probability of success. The United States Navy and Federal Express, to mention a couple of companies, have used the concept successfully.

Application to Six Sigma

While using this tool several years ago it seemed that this would be a great application and tool to measure, monitor and improve both the alignment and behaviours of an organization implementing Six Sigma. In "troubleshooting" issues with a Six Sigma deployment, imagine if you had a database with responses from hundreds or even thousands of employees. Imagine if you had statistical data that showed you that "Black Belts were adequately trained in all appropriate skills", "Senior Management was engaged" but "Champions were not." Then you could sort by Division or Plant to see if the behaviours were Companywide or isolated. This example illustrates how an organization could effectively drive very pointed actions over time using this concept.

With the proliferation of web based tools, measuring, managing and improving with data has become easier and much more efficient. If your organization, large or small, has a Six Sigma program in place, you should be measuring your return on investment (ROI) and determining whether or not it is achieving the benchmark levels mentioned at the beginning of this chapter. If it's not, consider what your Six Sigma Critical Success Factors are, and ask how you are doing against them. Further, ask how you are measuring them and using them to drive optimization. I guarantee that if you are not getting benchmark results from your Six Sigma process, the definition, management and optimization of the Critical Success Factors are the place to look.

Universal Critical Success Factors

Accepting the General Electric definition of Six Sigma as "completely satisfying customers' needs profitably" means that Six Sigma requires a company-wide initiative to dramatically improve process performance. It means that every employee in a company learns a structured approach to managing improvement projects and solving problems using facts and taking the customer's perspective. It means on-target performance with minimum variation. With those givens in mind, here are some of the factors of Six Sigma which are considered universal.

1. Clear Project Chartering and Sponsorship
Defining the business case for the project, scope, baseline measures, resources required, potential risks and naming a senior executive as mentor/sponsor for the life of the project.

2. Identification of Customers and Their Needs
Identifying who receives the outcome of the process and what is critical to quality from their perspective.

3. Application of Measures
Describing the outcomes (Ys), process and input (x's) measures upon which the project will focus.

4. Analysis of Causal Variables
Using quantitative methods to define causal relationships and the vital few variables that impact the desired outcome.

5. Improvement of Mean Performance and Sigma
Levels Reducing variability, not just average performance.

6. Standardization and Application of Control Charts
Putting in place the tools to track performance on an ongoing basis.

Case studies of two European companies show how they successfully maintained these foundation elements yet adapted Six Sigma to their national and company cultures.

Siemens

Business Improvement with Six Sigma as Toolkit
Siemens is an example of a German multinational company that carefully thought through its approach to Six Sigma, with a focus on improving collective business performance. Important to Siemens was how Six Sigma fits with other improvement initiatives such as ISO 9000 or the European Foundation for Quality Management (EFQM) Business Excellence

Model. Not one to take on the "flavour of the month," Siemens carefully assessed what contribution Six Sigma could make and integrated it into a comprehensive, logical approach to improvement called Top+ Quality.

The benefit of the Siemens approach is the top-down link to business improvement objectives, the distinction between process/input levers and other levers which are important but not suited for Six Sigma, and finally the highlighting of senior management's role throughout the process. By positioning Six Sigma as a toolkit in a larger improvement methodology, Siemens concentrates on overall business improvement and effectiveness.

Ericsson

A Vehicle for Individual and Organizational Change

Ericsson is a Swedish multinational that is an example of a company Ericsson whose approach to Six Sigma balances the needs of the company with the needs of the individuals on whose support success depends. Because implementing Six Sigma often entails radical changes, receptivity to change for an individual as well as an organization is an important predictor of success.

In addition, because Ericsson recognizes the need to engage on the individual level, it designed its Six Sigma training with an opportunity for "contracting" between project leaders and their managers. The manager of each participant in a Six Sigma Black Belt course attends one day during the first week of training. This gives time off-line for the manager to clarify a number of critical elements, why the person was selected, why the project was chosen, how the success or failure of the project will affect the individual's career. Likewise, the project leader can negotiate for the time needed to work on the project assignment and the support he/she will need from the supervisor. Particularly in companies where Black Belts are balancing project work with operational responsibilities, contracting for time to work on assignments is vital to the success of Six Sigma.

Ericsson demystified change in measurable and practical terms. By weaving change management modules and contracting sessions into Six Sigma training Ericsson significantly increased the probability of success.

Uncompromising yet Flexible

Bedrock principles of Six Sigma should not to be compromised regardless of the country. However, to be successful, a company has to fit Six Sigma into the organizational and cultural context in which it is working. In Germany, support for Six Sigma is gained by showing how it relates to an integrated concept of improvement. This includes acknowledging the value of existing approaches, and clarifying both the ultimate goal and the steps for getting there. In Scandinavia, the focus must be on the individual and the benefits that Six Sigma offers him/her. This includes de-emphasizing "stretch goals" imposed from above, communicating the personal development the individual acquires through Six Sigma, and acknowledging and working with the factors that influence the capability to change.

The art of successfully implementing Six Sigma is to be uncompromising about the critical ingredients for success while being flexible to the cultural context in which one is working.

Chapter 13: Driving Six Sigma Success without Top-level Support

If practitioners are having trouble attracting executive backing for Six Sigma, there are four steps that can help point a deployment in the right direction.

Common wisdom about Six Sigma is that top-level executive support is one of the prerequisites for having a successful deployment, regardless of the organization. Almost all Six Sigma training materials (either developed in-house or delivered by external consultants) for Green Belts and Black Belts focuses extensively on how executive support is critical for the success of a Six Sigma program or project in particular.

However, the reality is that many organizations today have Six Sigma programs that never extend beyond mid-level management. At best, these programs are merely tolerated by top leadership or, even worse, totally ignored by upper executives until the program fails on its own.

In many cases a departmental manager who is Six Sigma-savvy and has seen the first-hand benefits of the methodology might hire a Black Belt to drive projects without having the right infrastructure or visible top-level commitment. While this scenario is not ideal for Six Sigma success, it does not necessarily mean that the Belt is set up for failure.

By adopting the following strategies, Belts can not only complete projects successfully, but also ultimately build a successful Six Sigma program that gets sufficient top level recognition and support.

Step 1: Establish your Proof of Concept

If the project is not important to the company's operations or business there is little chance that the project will succeed. Thankfully, no manager in their right frame of mind would dedicate an expensive Six Sigma resource to a project that is not critical to the business goals. However, the onus is on the Belt to ensure that the first project is scoped properly, has significant improvement targets and can be completed with a short turnaround time.

Successful completion of such high-impact projects almost always generates tremendous excitement and, ultimately, top-level commitment to building a sustainable Six Sigma program. Once the Belt has a successful project completed, he or she can then be more careful in identifying future projects and maintaining momentum within the business. Personally, I have been involved with programs where leadership perception changed from passive tolerance to active support based on the success of a single major Six Sigma project. Remember: Nothing succeeds like success.

Step 2: Build a Team with the Right Individuals

Most Six Sigma projects depend on a team; it is extremely rare to come across a project that was accomplished by the Belt alone. On the other hand, without top-level support it can be extremely difficult to secure the necessary time and commitment from the team members. The only way to overcome the lack of senior-level support is by picking a project that is a pain point for all the team members and is directly related to their work and area of influence.

Practitioners must build a team of individuals who feel the need for change, and also have the ability and desire ("what's in it for me?") to make changes. This task is not as difficult as it sounds; most businesses have some broken processes that adversely affect all departments of an organization, but have not been addressed because members of the cross-functional team have learned to accept them. Picking one of these broken processes as the initial project should ultimately ensure sufficient commitment from all team members and improve the odds of project success. This experience also will make it much easier to recruit team members for future projects.

Step 3: Demystify Six Sigma

Because not all Six Sigma programs have been successful over the years, there are some senior-level business leaders who understandably have a bad impression of Six Sigma. However, almost all of the failures they cite have come about due to problems with execution of the methodology rather than the methodology itself. Poor choice of Belts, improper training, poor selection of projects or team members, improper scoping, and other factors all have contributed to the failure of Six Sigma programs.

When dealing with these "once bitten, twice shy" organizations, it is important for the Belt to stay away from overly technical jargon and confusing acronyms. Instead, they should make the whole process as easily understandable as possible to the rest of the organization. Some practitioners have even consciously stayed away from calling their program "Six Sigma." Only after they get a successful project under the belt should they begin to educate internal employees about standard Six Sigma terminology, approaches and structures.

Step 4: Be your own Champion

Take the time to meet individually with mid and senior-level management and talk about their biggest pain points to determine how you can offer to solve them. You may wish to take on projects without calling your methods Six Sigma, but be sure to follow the structured Six Sigma approach; when the project is completed, you must be able to establish that the success was attributable to the methodology.

All companies and business leaders like good press, especially when projects are completed with validated improvements. Once your project is finished, take this opportunity to share the achievement by making use of internal newsletters, websites, blogs and any other forms of communication, including external resources and publications. Try to rope in fellow team members and other employees to share the benefits of the methodology. Find out which of these colleagues will be most able to convey the project's success to the organization in order to develop a vested interest from corporate leadership.

Even without top-level support, a Six Sigma program can be successfully established and eventually maintained in an organization. However, in order to achieve these goals, it is important to select the right project, have the right team, tone down the technical jargon and acronyms, and communicate your successful results once the first project is completed

Chapter 14: Eight Lessons for Success in Lean Six Sigma Deployment

An uncounted number of corporate executives around the world have been quoted as saying: "General Electric has been extremely successful in its implementation of Six Sigma, but we are not GE!"

Indeed, each company is unique. And it is questionable whether Jack Welch, the former head of GE at the time the company implemented Six Sigma so successfully, could have achieved the same results in many non-U.S.-based companies, considering the differences in culture and social legislations from country to country. Among the many companies that have embarked on the Six Sigma journey, some have achieved spectacular success while others have failed. What makes the difference? Here are eight lessons learned from some of those successes and failures.

Lesson 1: Six Sigma must be Integrated with Lean

Six Sigma techniques are powerful in reducing process variation but are unable to significantly improve process speed. Lean tools and techniques are specifically designed to reduce wasted time in a process. Today, an increasing number of companies are implementing a combined Lean Six Sigma approach to business excellence.

Lesson 2: Lean Six Sigma Efforts Must Support Business Objectives

Successful deployments are based on a "burning platform" – some major business challenge or risk that the company can overcome only through Lean Six Sigma. It could be a need to regain competitiveness in the market, a need to introduce new services, attract new customers, retain existing customers or simply improve profitability. Identifying a burning platform means all the company's business leaders are clear about why the company is adopting strategies based on Lean Six Sigma principles. It also means that decisions about the use of Lean Six Sigma methods will be driven by the question: "Will doing this support or detract from our business goals?" Above all else, the CEO and other executives must speak with one voice about the burning platform for their business.

Lesson 3: Key Executives Must Be Engaged in the Process

Two years into a Lean Six Sigma deployment, one company did a review on its progress to date. The review included interviews with key decision makers throughout the organization. One of the more revealing interviews came from the vice president of product development a key player in the organization. First, the R & D Director said, he had not been invited to attend any Six Sigma training, nor had any Champions or Black Belts asked him about his priorities. Second, he and his staff were keenly aware of all the money and effort being devoted to the

Black Belts. The R & D Director and his staff had absolutely no reason to actively support Six Sigma, and instead had grown to view it with some resentment. By ignoring the importance of their commitment and support, the organization missed a prime opportunity to capitalize on all its resources.

Managers will never fully support Lean Six Sigma if they view it as taking away from their resources rather than adding capability and helping them become more successful in achieving their goals; nor will they actively support it if they think it is eating up vital budgetary allotments rather than setting the stage for significant financial payback. To avoid such pitfalls, a company must involve all key business leaders in helping to design its Lean Six Sigma deployment. By giving them a voice in project selection, priorities and ongoing monitoring, an organization can be assured of their commitment to the effort.

Lesson 4: Develop a Project Selection Process Based on Value Potential

If a company asks employees and customers for improvement suggestions, it will end up with many more ideas than it can possibly act on. The worst way to select which of these ideas to implement is to look at who made the suggestion, giving priority to ideas contributed by senior managers or ideas that are supported by a majority of leaders or employees.

The most effective Lean Six Sigma companies have a rigorous project selection process driven by an evaluation of how much shareholder value a project can generate. It can be characterized as a trade-off decision comparing value delivered to effort expended.

Lesson 5: Find the Critical Mass of Projects and Resources

Some companies start their deployments by training a handful of people and launching a few "demonstration" projects. Others ramp-up for immediate corporate-wide deployment, training hundreds of Black Belts and launching dozens of projects within the first six months. Either approach is workable, but for every company there is a critical level of Lean Six Sigma effort; below that level, projects and focus eventually fade away. Above that level, excitement and momentum build into a sustainable advantage.

Lesson 6: Actively Manage Projects-in-Process

Given that most companies want to generate measurable, significant results within six months or a year, the tendency is to push as many projects into the Lean Six Sigma deployment as possible. But one of the most important lessons that Lean principles teach is that pushing excess work into a process slows down the process and dramatically increases lead times. As Lean practitioners know, results can be speeded up by reducing the amount of work in process per Black Belt. That means controlling the number of active projects at any given time. It is better to focus on getting a few high-potential projects done right than to just flood the workplace with dozens of less-important projects. With the right resources working on the right projects, learning and results are maximized by short cycle times.

Lesson 7: Emphasize Team Leadership Skills

Use of Lean Six Sigma does involve some technical skills; the ability to process and analyze data, for example. But good leadership skills are even more important. This has been especially true in Europe, where differences among team members are compounded by differences among regional, national and cross-border cultures. This emphasis on leadership also relates to how a company chooses people to fill Black Belt roles. Placing the most promising operations people in the Black Belt role is painful at first, yet it yields fast results and a rapid transformation of the organization.

Lesson 8: Track Results Rigorously

Lean Six Sigma results should "pay as you go" and be confirmed by objective parties. Too many companies discount the necessity of having a reliable means to judge project results and impact, or they underestimate the difficulty in creating such a system. Lean Six Sigma results must be quantified so a company can appropriately evaluate their impact and make good decisions about whether resources are being used wisely. A senior level finance person should participate in the development of a results-tracking rule book.

As a deployment is planned, a company must think in terms of leading measurements or key performance indicators of the potential financial results. At a minimum, project cycle times and project values must be measured on a regular basis and to gain an understanding of the level of variation in these numbers. Once a company gains more experience, it likely will want to track a wider variety of metrics.

Chapter 15: Is Process Management Right for your Business?

A process can be defined as a set of ordered actions that lead to an output. In any business function, a goal is achieved through a process; pay cheques are printed, orders are taken, employees are hired. How well the processes operate is the focus of this chapter, and the focus of process management.

Process management involves the concept of defining macro and micro processes, assigning ownership, creating responsibilities for the owners who control the processes, and measuring the performance of each process. What are these processes? They are the processes that control what the customer receives or comes in contact with. (Remember, the customer may be internal as well as external).

Functional Structure Example

Let's take a simple example of a credit card company that primarily conducts business and acquires customers on the Internet.

If they were structuring their business as many others have done in the past, the following functions would be organized in the business: marketing/sales, operations, human resources, finance, legal, business development, and many others. Each function views themselves as an individual silo with individual

91

requirements, inputs and outputs. As a result of this structure, each silo manager is rewarded by the performance of their individual group not necessarily the performance that leads to customer benefit.

Process Management Structure Example

A process management focused organization takes a slightly different structure. The first interaction is the customer becoming aware of the business, so publicity may be the first macro process management step of our fictitious business. Key measurements might include customer targeting, click through rate of banners or other media, budgetary effectiveness, etc.

Publicity Start: Customer views media.

Publicity Stop: Customer enters company Web site through media.

If the marketing media is effective enough to draw a customer to the credit card company's Web site, the next step of the process might involve educating the customer on the who/what/where/why/how's of your products and services. It would be measured by how understandable the Web site content is, how well you can quickly sell to the customer, and how easy and time consuming it is to complete an application. Let's call this macro process management step conversion.

Conversion Start: Customer enters company Web site through media.

Conversion Stop: Customer exits Web site or submits application for a credit card.

Once an application is accepted by the business (of course, it is poka yoke'd before acceptance to ensure the customer has checked the application for typos, a credit check is performed, and that in general it is a customer that the business wants), it must be processed. We'll call this macro process management step processing. It involves printing the plastic cards, a welcome letter, terms and conditions for use, packaging, and of course a packet of cross sell materials for other products. Key metrics might include turn-around time from application acceptance to receipt by customer, accuracy of information, accuracy of cross sell information based on customer credit profile, etc.

Processing Start: Customer submits application for credit card.

Processing Stop: Customer receives credit card and welcome materials.

When a customer receives the welcome package, they activate their card via the telephone and begin charging. They also receive statements in the mail summarizing their usage, they have questions and interact with the company for support, they may lose their cards, or perform a host of other activities.

This macro process management step involves all the servicing of the customer. Servicing is measured by the customer in terms of how quickly their concern is addressed, how completely it is resolved, the level of competency of company representatives, and many others.

Servicing Start: Customer receives credit card and welcome materials.

Servicing Stop: Customer terminates account.

Of course the company hopes that the processing process never ends, as that means they lose a customer.

You can see how the processes are assembled as customer experience them and they are measured as the customer 'feels' the process, not as the business decides to measure their own performance. Why should the customer bend to the way we perform our processes? After all, it is the customer that is paying our salaries!

Just as the credit card business has four macro process management steps, each of these steps may have two, four or even 12 sub process steps. These sub process steps may operate in series or parallel or both. Other functions such as human resources, legal and finance are intertwined with the process and sub process steps to achieve the end result.

With process management, everyone wins in the end the employee, the business and especially the customer. Implementation is the key; you may be up against decades of cultural brainwashing, and change is often times difficult to accept. But when properly implemented and coupled with Six Sigma DMAIC and DMADV projects to drive metrics, it is unbelievable.

Competition watch out!

Chapter 16: Successful Six Sigma Deployment

Six Sigma deployment success is built on an infrastructure foundation. Learn to align projects to business strategy, and use a balanced DMAIC framework as your key to successful Six Sigma deployment.

All Six Sigma proponents agree to the fact that the key to Six Sigma improvement success is the building up of an effective infrastructure. An effective infrastructure lays the foundation for the success of the organization in its implementation of Six Sigma. It is a known fact today that the success of Six Sigma lays on the projects selected and their link to the strategy of their organization. There have been enough publications on the selection of projects and the filters to be used for the prioritization of projects, however there are not enough details available on the building the key infrastructure for the deployment of Six Sigma.

When we discuss the building up of an implementation structure what we are embarking on is a project in itself, which follows the DMAIC (Define, Measure, Analyze, Improve and Control) methodology:

1. D: Define the Strategic Direction of the organization.
2. M: Set Measures for the strategic objectives of the organization.

3. A: On a continual basis collect data on the measures set and analyse using Six Sigma tools and techniques.
4. I: Identify the opportunities for improvement and convert them to Six Sigma projects for improvement.
5. C: Set up a management control action of continuous reviews on the improvements made on the Six Sigma Projects.

The objectives of the Define and Measure phase of this project are defined as below:
1. Building up a set of metrics for the organization that give definition to the organizations Vision
2. Metrics that are Integrated with the Strategic direction and objectives of the organization
3. Metrics that align people and work with their strategic objectives
4. Metrics that serve as effective means of communication for the organization both horizontally and vertically.
5. Metrics that provide insight needed for making decisions, setting direction and correcting course.
6. Metrics which will serve as a continuous source for identifying gaps in the organization and plugging them with Six Sigma Projects

The problem most organizations face in the phases of Define and Measure is how to build such an organizational dashboard, which will help achieve the objectives cited above.

First Step

The first step an organization needs to embark on is conducting a self-assessment based on proven assessment models which will help the organization in understanding its "as is" state more clearly and help identify the various opportunities for improvement. The organizations could use the checklist type of approach in conjunction with interviews for identifying the gaps in Approach-Deployment-Results. Once the assessment of the organization is completed the findings need to be shared with the top management and the employees. This step is extremely crucial as this is what binds the organization together and helps create the cultural change needed aspect within the organization combined with the need for Six Sigma.

Second Step

Once the first step is conducted the organization is now clear about its current strategies for growth and customer satisfaction. Based on the assessment conducted the organization can re-evaluate all its strategies and strategic objectives. New strategic objectives can now be identified.

Third Step

Most organizations after having articulated and identified their various objectives are unable to communicate the strategies of the organization. One of the most effective methods for communicating the strategy of the organization is building a strategy map encompassing the now widely adopted Kaplan and Norton's Balanced score card spanning the four perspectives. Answering the questions related to the perspectives helps understand the strategy better and also build a good strategy map. The strategy map helps provide the vital cause and effect linkages in an organization and helps link the Business processes to the strategic destination of the organization. Before attempting to build the map it is essential for the organization to identify all its core processes and support processes as they help in completing the strategy map.

Fourth Step

Once the strategy map is completed the organization can now start looking at each of the objectives in the shareholders and customer perspectives, and identify various measures that will help in achieving the strategy. When identifying measures, organizations must try to focus on what needs to be measured to achieve the strategy rather than plug existing measures into the objectives. Measures selected need to have a right balance between Lead and Lag. Lag measures are metrics that are obtained after the event is over, whereas Lead measures are metrics that tend to measure the drivers that help reach the destination.

Identify the various benchmarks in the Industry for the various measures selected. Based on the current level of performance decide on targets for the organization.

Fifth Step

For the key core and support processes, develop high level process maps based on the concept of SIPOC (Supplier, Input, Process, Output and Customer). The process model developed earlier serves as an excellent resource. Identify key metrics for each of these processes. Return back to the strategy map developed and for each of the process strategic objectives select appropriate measures linking both the customer perspective measures identified in step four to the process perspective measures identified. Select process strategic objectives measures that reflect the customer's viewpoint. Conventional Six Sigma metrics like DPMO, Sigma Level, or Rolled Throughput Yield may be appropriate. Once the measures for the process strategic objectives are identified, identify measures for the learning and growth perspectives. As discussed earlier, remember to balance in Lead and Lag measures and identify suitable benchmarks for these measures.

Sixth Step

Deploy the organizational score card at the departmental level. During the deployment of the scorecard break up the measures as applicable to the department. This would ensure that the organization has appropriate metrics at all levels and that they are integrated both vertically and horizontally within the organization.

Seventh Step

Once the organization is hardwired with the metrics, start collecting data on the metrics and identify on a continual basis various gaps in the organization. The champions training received by the Senior Management will be extremely useful in this phase as the champions will analyse data based on the type of cause (special or common) and then would work on whether a potential project is identified or not.

An implementation structure of Six Sigma modelled on this method is a sure fire method for ensuring maximum benefits from the Six Sigma strategy deployed within the organization.

"When you can measure what you are speaking about and express it in numbers you know something about it, but when you cannot measure it, when you cannot express it in numbers, your knowledge is of a meagre and unsatisfactory kind." –Lord Kelvin

Develop Correct Six Sigma Project Metrics

One of the crucial elements of the project charter in the define phase of a Six Sigma project is the selection of project metrics. Proper project metrics should reflect more than just business and customer measurable.

One of the crucial elements of the project charter in the define phase of a Six Sigma project is the selection of project metrics. Project metrics selected should reflect the voice of the customer (customer needs), as well as ensure that the internal metrics selected by the organization are achieved. Metrics selected should be simple and straightforward and meaningful. Metrics selected should create a common language among diverse team members.

When drafting metrics for a particular project one should consider how the metrics are connected and related to key business metrics. Typically there is no one metric that fits all the requirements for a particular situation.

Developing Project Metrics

The most common approach used by teams is to understand the problem statement, brainstorm metrics, and finally decide what metrics can help them achieve better performance. The team then reviews these metrics with executive management to ensure that they are in synergy with the overall strategy of the business, and an iterative approach may be utilized.

Care should be exercised in determining what is measured. Metrics should be based on what, in fact, needs to be measured to improve the process, rather than what fits the current measurement system. Metrics need to be scrutinized from the value they add in understanding a process.

Balanced Scorecard Approach to Metrics

Many Six Sigma professionals advocate the use of a Balanced Scorecard type of approach for the selection of project metrics as a method for ensuring that the project meets both customer and business needs. The Balanced Scorecard approach includes both financial and non-financial metrics, as well as lagging and leading measures across the four areas or perspectives: Financial, Customer, Internal Processes, and Employee Learning and Growth. Lagging measures are those that are measured at the end of an event, while leading measures are measures that help as achieve the objectives and are measured upstream of the event.

Most Balanced Scorecard metrics are based on brainstorming; however the approach of brainstorming can have limited success in establishing sound metrics that have a good balance between lagging and leading measures.

Typical brainstormed Balanced Scorecard metrics utilized in Six Sigma projects can be summarized below. The primary issue in utilizing a scorecard is that it might not reflect the actual strategies applied by the team for achieving breakthrough in their project.

Example Project Balanced Scorecard
1. Financial
2. Inventory Levels
3. Cost Per Unit
4. Hidden Factory
5. Activity Based Costing
6. Cost of Poor Quality
7. Overall Project Savings
8. Customer

Customer Satisfaction
1. On Time Delivery
2. Final Product Quality
3. Safety Communications

Internal Business Processes
1. Defects, Inspection Data, DPMO, Sigma Level
2. Rolled Throughput Yield
3. Supplier Quality
4. Cycle Time
5. Volume Shipped
6. Rework Hours

Employee Learning and Growth
1. Six Sigma Tool Utilization
2. Quality of Training
3. Meeting Effectiveness
4. Lessons Learned
5. Total Trained in Six Sigma
6. Project Schedule versus Actual Date
7. Number of Projects Completed
8. Total Savings to Date

Once the team has brainstormed for each of the four perspectives, the various objectives that must be met by the project will be clearer. These objectives can then be mapped in a strategy map cutting across all the perspectives and projects of the organization.

Once the strategy map for the project is determined, the team can begin brainstorming appropriate metrics for each of the objectives and, while doing so, maintain a balance in selection between leading and lagging measures. This kind of an approach ensures that the team selects a set of metrics that are aligned with the strategy used by them on the Six Sigma Project. Metrics selected in this way not only ensure that appropriate metrics are developed but also help the team in the project planning and creates a purpose of direction for the team.

Chapter 17: Aligning Six Sigma with Objectives and Strategies

In a well-managed business that has implemented Six Sigma, the organization's objectives and strategies and continuous improvement are all closely aligned. Organizational objectives enhance the efficacy and importance of Six Sigma initiatives. And Six Sigma specialists can play an integral role in ensuring the execution of strategy.

In many organizations, however, there seems to be great confusion between strategy and objectives. Senior-level strategy meetings, as rare as they are in organizations, are often disrupted by the topic of objectives and, as a result, an understanding of corporate strategy is never realized. The execution of strategy is necessary for an organization to get to the place where it desires to be. Without an understanding of strategy, execution becomes impossible.

Strategy versus Objectives

So what is the difference between strategy and objectives?

Objectives are the goals that the organization strives to achieve. They are reflected in performance metrics, strategic plans, mission statements and anyplace where employees need reminding of the importance of their work. The strategy is the action plan that is going to enable the organization to achieve its objectives. As an example of the relationship between objectives and strategies, here is an objective and its companion strategy:

Objective:

Increase the number of e-newsletter subscribers who sign up online each week by 15 percent.

Strategy:

Make signing up for the e-newsletter online a one-step process, instead of a process that requires a signup step followed a confirmation step later when the e-newsletter arrives. (And the success of the strategy will be measured by comparing the average number of new subscribers each week for the three months before the process change to the number of new subscribers each week for the three months after the change.)

Too often strategies are not executed because they are not understood. According to the Balanced Scorecard Collaborative, an educational, training, research and development firm, nine out of ten companies fail to implement strategies and 85 percent of executive teams spend less than one hour per month discussing strategy. With this lack of regard for strategy, it is no wonder as to why organizations do not achieve their objectives.

But when an organization is able to clearly establish its strategy, the entire process of implementation begins with the communication of strategy through senior leadership. Senior management must communicate the strategy to the organization, justify the strategy and establish buy-in for the strategy. Communication is a process that begins with the top of the organization and goes to the bottom.

However, the actual process of strategy execution begins with the bottom of the organization. Employees within the organizational silos perform the activities that comprise the strategy. It is through the daily activities of employees that an organization can achieve its objectives. So, just as executives play a crucial role in formulating and communicating strategy, employees are essential in executing strategy.

The Strategic Role of Six Sigma

Organizational objectives can enhance the efficacy and importance of Six Sigma initiatives. While strategy is executed to achieve objectives, Six Sigma specialists can play an integral role in ensuring the execution of strategy.

Objectives can give the utmost priority to specific Six Sigma projects. For instance, if an organization wants to improve customer satisfaction by 25 percent, Six Sigma projects related to the voice of the customer can take priority and become an important part of the organizational strategy of achieving the customer-related objective. To become a part of strategy execution in this case, Six Sigma professionals could develop customer surveys, test questionnaires, gather customer data, analyze data and establish focus groups to name a few activities. Also, some old projects can be given new life through corporate objectives. Ideas for projects that have never been supported by a Champion can be reintroduced and possibly gain support through the relevance of new objectives. By letting organizational objectives align with Six Sigma projects, Six Sigma professionals can serve as leaders in showing employees how to execute strategy.

Also, to improve the process of Six Sigma project selection for Champions and Master Black Belts, Six Sigma professionals can align the needs established by organizational objectives with Pareto's Principle, or the 80-20 rule. Through incorporating factors such as savings, probability of success, cost and time of completion, Six Sigma professionals can find the essential 20 percent of projects that can generate 80 percent of the results that are necessary for achieving objectives. While objectives can guide Six Sigma professionals to the right type of projects, logic-based premises such as Pareto's Principle can assist in the identification of the specific projects that are necessary for success.

While Six Sigma professionals are traditionally known for demonstrating cost savings, they also should be regarded as those who execute strategy. By building the process of project selection around the most immediate organizational objectives, Six Sigma professionals can enhance the importance of their own work and optimize their contribution to the organization's success.

Chapter 18: Tips for Doing a Deployment Review

It is not unusual to find that a few years down the road, the results from a Lean Six Sigma deployment are not quite as good as what a company hoped or expected. What often helps in that situation is a formal deployment review, conducted in much the same way as a tollgate review on an individual project.

The basic model for a deployment review is the same as for any review. The organization's leadership will want to document both results and methods. This will make it clear whether progress has been hindered by a breakdown in strategy and planning (the methods), in the execution of those plans (the results) or a combination of both.

The methods the organization thought would be successful were not. Determine what went wrong Desired results obtained despite not following the planned methods. What was missing or wrong in the plans? What new knowledge allowed the organization to get good results?

Strategy Integration Review

To determining whether the organization had a clearly defined strategy associated with its Lean Six Sigma deployment, and whether both the hard and soft results are documented.

Method Questions

1. What was the burning platform driving Lean Six Sigma deployment?
2. Was the strategic importance of the goals clearly communicated to all involved?
3. Was progress regularly reviewed against the goals?
4. How does the organization ensure that project selection is driven by priority business needs?

Results Questions

1. Is there reliable data on performance before and after changes were made? (Sometimes good results are obscured by poor data collection; or vice versa, bad results can look good if data is unreliable.)
2. What documentation does the organization have showing progress toward or shortfalls relating to strategic goals?

Skilled Infrastructure Review

What has made Lean Six Sigma much more successful than its predecessors is having an implementation infrastructure that effectively translates the strategic agenda into actions to maximize value and provide effective management and monitoring of results.

Method Questions

1. Is there a deployment Champion in each business unit? What training and experience does he or she have?
2. Have project Sponsors been trained in Lean Six Sigma basics and project review basics?

3. How good are the mechanisms in place for connecting resources working in terms of support and communication? What is the basis for this judgment?
4. What evidence does the organization have that Lean Six Sigma is becoming integrated into the daily management practices of the business?
5. What is being done to ensure that deployed resources are carrying out their responsibilities? (For example, are they held accountable for both methods and sustainable results?)

Results Questions
1. What targets for achieving a critical mass were set around the deployment methods? (Number of Black Belts trained? Number of projects launched?) How do the actual numbers compare to the target? What barriers explain any shortfalls?
2. Is there a rigorous process for measurement and tracking of project financial results?
3. What is the average return per Black Belt? How does that compare to expectations?

Execution Review

The first two elements of the deployment review focused on developing a fully realized strategy and the resources to implement it. In this element, an organization needs to look at where and how execution either succeeded or failed.

Method Questions

1. What made the organization confident that its expectations were reasonable? Check that those factors are still valid. If it turns out the expectations were un-reasonable, what needs to change; the expectations or the methods used to fulfil them?

2. What was done to engage leadership and give them a compelling reason to embrace Lean Six Sigma?

3. Were Black Belts and Green Belts fully trained in integrated Lean Six Sigma DMAIC methodology?

4. Is team leadership training a standard part of the organization's Lean Six Sigma curriculum? (Change and improvement happen through people, not just statistical tools. Black Belts and Champions must be able to draw the best from their teams. This requires that they be trained in team leadership skills as well as technical tools. Having the right teams and team dynamics in place for learning and execution can both accelerate the application of Lean Six Sigma and multiply its financial and operational benefits throughout an organization.)

5. How are Champions and Master Black Belts doing in terms of opportunity identification, project selection, and prioritization? How does the organization's leadership know?

6. Does the organization have a project management system that allows it to control numbers of projects-in-progress so that staff is not overloaded?

7. Have project Sponsors taken on the accountability for long-term results? What indicators are there that this is happening or not? Is there a method for financial validation of results after projects are completed?
8. Is there consensus on common metrics and tracking methods? What dashboards metrics are reviewed regularly? Are they helping in the management of the deployment?

Results Questions

1. What hard results were expected from the deployment (quality, cost, profit, revenue, speed, etc.)?
2. What results were actually achieved?
3. How well do team leaders, Black Belts, Master Black Belts, etc. rate in terms of leadership skills?

Who Reviews and When

Keep in mind, that although each of these elements was addressed separately, in reality there will be overlap between them. That is okay because organizations typically will compile all the lessons together at the end so they can look for patterns across elements. If progress is not being made toward strategic goals, for example, it could be that there is a problem with project selection and prioritization, the numbers of projects launched and completed, or the resources used to support the projects (such as if Black Belt time is limited).

In practice, these reviews are often done through a combination of meetings (with the leadership team, Champions, Sponsors, Master Black Belts, etc.), reviews of project documentation, and internal surveys or focus groups that ask people about barriers and successes.

Most best-in-class companies perform in-depth deployment reviews annually. The trick is to find a balance between getting enough depth so that big course corrections can be made when needed, but not spending so much time and effort that it slows down the initiative. The stakes are high, so spending time and money on doing a good review is well worth the effort.

Chapter 19: 5 Six Sigma Deployment Mistakes and How to Avoid Them

A well planned Six Sigma deployment can lead to a rewarding experience and immense benefits for an organization. On the flip side, however, a flawed deployment may lead to disappointing results, the failure of the entire deployment effort, and/or a significant waste of time and resources. There are five problems in Six Sigma deployments, which, if not handled well, will derail a deployment effort. By recognizing these mistakes and working to avoid them, a team can stay on track.

Problem 1: Leadership Indifference

Support and commitment for a Six Sigma deployment from the leadership of an organization is the key driver for success. Leadership must walk the talk and continuously emphasize the importance of Six Sigma at all forums. Support should be forthcoming not only from senior leadership, but also from leadership at all levels in the organization. No amount of good intentions, resources, effort or time will make up for missing sustained leadership support.

Solutions

Because this support is such a driver, extra effort should be made to keep leadership engaged at all stages in the organization's Six Sigma journey. Senior management should share regular communications with the entire organization, emphasizing the importance of the Six Sigma initiative and how it is tied to the organization's overall business objectives. Senior management should also reserve time to review deployment progress at all management review meetings and should be careful in granting their team any concessions on Six Sigma goals. It is important for Six Sigma to be a compulsory agenda item for all the public events in the organization as well.

Problem 2: Faulty Deployment Strategy

A deployment strategy helps to align organizational business goals to expected deployment results and to maintain the sustenance of Six Sigma in the organization. Lack of alignment may cause confusion among the key stakeholders and associates about the value of the entire effort; this gap delays deployment in many organizations.

Solutions

To avoid this, Six Sigma deployment strategies must align the organization's business goals with the deployment results. Strategies should encompass all aspects of deployment planning, Six Sigma learning and development within the organization, project execution and coaching, information management, and operational excellence achievement. Teams should evaluate their progress on each of the strategies at regular intervals and tie it to a change in business results.

Once this relationship is established, teams may start monitoring the relationship closely, regularly sharing the information on change in business results with the organization and conducting any course correction if required. Visible change in business results gives an organization confidence in the Six Sigma effort.

Problem 3: Stress on Training and Certification

Training and certification are important aspects of an overall Six Sigma deployment effort because they build competency within the organization. But sometimes teams are more focused on training and certification goals, and fail to support project execution. Without adequate mentoring and coaching support after their initial training, Belts may select projects simply to meet the certification targets or projects may be inordinately delayed.

Solution

Deployment teams should always be focused on the organization's business goals and create an infrastructure for Six Sigma project selection, mentoring and coaching that will bring the most tangible benefits for the organization. To stay on track, senior management should regularly review changes in business results along with parameters of the Six Sigma deployment such as training and certification, and insist on course correction if there is lack of progress on business results.

Problem 4: Incorrect Project Selection

A lack of focus on project selection and prioritization can lead to projects that lack data or business focus or projects focused on process areas that are outside the Green Belts' and Black Belts' realm of control. This results in delayed or scrapped projects, and quick disillusionment among the Green Belts and Black Belts.

Solution

Deployment teams must ensure that selected Six Sigma process improvement projects are data-based and focused on business, financial, process and customer goals, and prioritized properly to ensure these goals are met. Teams should conduct regular workshops for project identification and selection, and ensure that all selected projects have a sponsor who will be responsible for tracking and signing off the business benefits of the Six Sigma project. Once the projects are in progress, teams should closely monitor progress, provide additional mentoring if required and make corrections if business goals are not being met.

Problem 5: Segregating the Effort

Every individual member of an organization has a stake in its growth and progress; therefore, each is responsible for contributing to and facilitating a successful deployment. Yet sometimes deployment teams fail to communicate the benefits of the Six Sigma deployment to the key stakeholders. Often only the deployment team will make formal goals relating to Six Sigma results.

Solutions

Teams should link together an organization's business and strategic goals, Six Sigma deployment goals and individual goals to explain to the rest of the organization how everything is closely related. This way they may win support from all the associates in the organization which they need to meet the deployment goals. Senior management should regularly reach out to their organization's associates about the importance of deployment results and how the results can benefit their careers; career growth is a powerful booster for deployment initiatives. In addition, senior leadership and other associates at an organization, on whom Six Sigma success depends, also should set deployment goals. Deployment teams can help to chart out Six Sigma roadmaps for all the individuals in the organization to ensure that everybody is responsible for the deployment and monitoring the integration of Six Sigma into the company's DNA.

Fight Problems Early

Successfully avoiding these common mistakes will yield long-term benefits for an organization and accelerate its march toward becoming best in its class. The key to success is to identify these challenges early and take robust corrective actions to nip the problems before they become an issue. Leadership and organization support as well as a robust deployment strategy will help a team steer clear of these roadblocks and can create a win-win situation for all the key stakeholders in the organization.

Chapter 20: Six Sigma Unique Features

Features that set Six Sigma apart from previous quality improvement initiatives include:

1. A clear focus on achieving measurable and quantifiable financial returns from any Six Sigma project.
2. An increased emphasis on strong and passionate management leadership and support.
3. A special infrastructure of "Champions", "Master Black Belts", "Black Belts", "Green Belts", etc. to lead and implement the Six Sigma approach.
4. A clear commitment to making decisions on the basis of verifiable data, rather than assumptions and guesswork.

As mention earlier this book the term "Six Sigma" comes from a field of statistics known as process capability studies. Originally, it referred to the ability of manufacturing processes to produce a very high proportion of output within specification. Processes that operate with "six sigma quality" over the short term are assumed to produce long-term defect levels below 3.4 defects per million opportunities (DPMO). Six Sigma's implicit goal is to improve all processes to that level of quality or better.

In recent years, some practitioners have combined Six Sigma ideas with lean manufacturing to create a methodology named Lean Six Sigma which is what we are focusing on in this book. The Lean Six Sigma methodology views lean manufacturing, which addresses process flow and waste issues, and Six Sigma, with its focus on variation and design, as complementary disciplines aimed at promoting "business and operational excellence". Companies such as IBM use Lean Six Sigma to focus transformation efforts not just on efficiency but also on growth. It serves as a foundation for innovation throughout the organization, from manufacturing and software development to sales and service delivery functions.

Methods

Six Sigma projects follow two project methodologies inspired by Deming's Plan-Do-Check-Act Cycle. These methodologies, composed of five phases each, bear the acronyms DMAIC and DMADV.

DMAIC is used for projects aimed at improving an existing business process. DMAIC is pronounced as "duh-may-ick".

DMADV is used for projects aimed at creating new product or process designs. DMADV is pronounced as "duh-mad-vee".

DMAIC

The DMAIC project methodology has five phases: Define the problem, the voice of the customer, and the project goals, specifically.

Measure key aspects of the current process and collect relevant data.

Analyze the data to investigate and verify cause-and-effect relationships. Determine what the relationships are, and attempt to ensure that all factors have been considered. Seek out root cause of the defect under investigation.

Improve or optimize the current process based upon data analysis using techniques such as design of experiments, poka yoke or mistake proofing, and standard work to create a new, future state process. Set up pilot runs to establish process capability.

Control the future state process to ensure that any deviations from target are corrected before they result in defects. Implement control systems such as statistical process control, production boards, visual workplaces, and continuously monitor the process.

DMADV or DFSS

The DMADV project methodology, also known as DFSS ("Design For Six Sigma"), features five phases:
1. Define design goals that are consistent with customer demands and the enterprise strategy.
2. Measure and identify CTQs (characteristics that are Critical To Quality), product capabilities, production process capability, and risks.
3. Analyze to develop and design alternatives, create a high-level design and evaluate design capability to select the best design.

4. Design details, optimize the design, and plan for design verification. This phase may require simulations.
5. Verify the design, set up pilot runs, implement the production process and hand it over to the process owner(s).

Chapter 21: Quality Management Tools and Methods Used in Six Sigma

Within the individual phases of a DMAIC or DMADV project, Six Sigma utilizes many established quality-management tools that are also used outside of Six Sigma.

The following are overview of the main methods used.

1. 5 Whys
2. Analysis of variance
3. ANOVA Gauge R&R
4. Axiomatic design
5. Business Process Mapping
6. Cause & effects diagram (also known as fishbone or Ishikawa diagram)
7. Check sheet
8. Chi-squared test of independence and fits
9. Control chart
10. Correlation
11. Cost-benefit analysis
12. CTQ tree
13. Design of experiments
14. Failure mode and effects analysis (FMEA)
15. General linear model
16. Histograms
17. Pareto analysis
18. Pareto chart
19. Pick chart
20. Process capability

21. Quality Function Deployment (QFD)
22. Quantitative marketing research through use of Enterprise Feedback Management (EFM) systems
23. Regression analysis
24. Root cause analysis
25. Run charts
26. Scatter diagram
27. SIPOC analysis (Suppliers, Inputs, Process, Outputs, Customers)
28. Stratification
29. Taguchi methods
30. Taguchi Loss Function
31. TRIZ

Chapter 22: Six Sigma Implementation Roles

One key innovation of Six Sigma involves the "professionalizing" of quality management functions. Prior to Six Sigma, quality management in practice was largely relegated to the production floor and to statisticians in a separate quality department. Formal Six Sigma programs adopt a ranking terminology (similar to some martial arts systems) to define a hierarchy (and career path) that cuts across all business functions.

Six Sigma identifies several key roles for its successful implementation.

Executive Leadership includes the CEO and other members of top management. They are responsible for setting up a vision for Six Sigma implementation. They also empower the other role holders with the freedom and resources to explore new ideas for breakthrough improvements.

Champions take responsibility for Six Sigma implementation across the organization in an integrated manner. The Executive Leadership draws them from upper management. Champions also act as mentors to Black Belts.

Master Black Belts, identified by champions, act as in-house coaches on Six Sigma. They devote 100% of their time to Six Sigma. They assist champions and guide Black Belts and Green Belts. Apart from statistical tasks, they spend their time on ensuring consistent application of Six Sigma across various functions and departments.

Black Belts operate under Master Black Belts to apply Six Sigma methodology to specific projects. They devote 100% of their time to Six Sigma. They primarily focus on Six Sigma project execution, whereas Champions and Master Black Belts focus on identifying projects/functions for Six Sigma.

Green Belts are the employees who take up Six Sigma implementation along with their other job responsibilities, operating under the guidance of Black Belts.

Some organizations use additional belt colours, such as Yellow Belts, for employees that have basic training in Six Sigma tools and generally participate in projects and 'white belts' for those locally trained in the concepts but do not participate in the project team.

Certification Corporations such as early Six Sigma pioneers General Electric and Motorola developed certification programs as part of their Six Sigma implementation, verifying individuals' command of the Six Sigma methods at the relevant skill level (Green Belt, Black Belt etc.). Following this approach, many organizations in the 1990s started offering Six Sigma certifications to their employees.

Criteria for Green Belt and Black Belt certification vary; some companies simply require participation in a course and a Six Sigma project. There is no standard certification body, and different certification services are offered by various quality associations and other providers against a fee.

The American Society for Quality for example requires Black Belt applicants to pass a written exam and to provide a signed affidavit stating that they have completed two projects, or one project combined with three years' practical experience in the body of knowledge. The International Quality Federation offers an online certification exam that organizations can use for their internal certification programs; it is statistically more demanding than the ASQ certification.

Chapter 23: Criticism of Six Sigma

Role of consultants

The use of "Black Belts" as itinerant change agents has (controversially) fostered an industry of training and certification. Critics argue there is overselling of Six Sigma by too great a number of consulting firms, many of which claim expertise in Six Sigma when they have only a rudimentary understanding of the tools and techniques involved.

Potential negative effects

A Fortune article stated that "of 58 large companies that have announced Six Sigma programs, 91 percent have trailed the S&P 500 since". The statement was attributed to "an analysis by Charles Holland of consulting firm Qualpro (which espouses a competing quality-improvement process)."The summary of the article is that Six Sigma is effective at what it is intended to do, but that it is "narrowly designed to fix an existing process" and does not help in "coming up with new products or disruptive technologies." Advocates of Six Sigma have argued that many of these claims are in error or ill-informed.

A more direct criticism is the "rigid" nature of Six Sigma with its over-reliance on methods and tools. In most cases, more attention is paid to reducing variation and less attention is paid to developing robustness (which can altogether eliminate the need for reducing variation).

Articles featuring critics appeared in the November-December 2006 issue of USA Army Logistician regarding Six-Sigma.

"The dangers of a single paradigmatic orientation (in this case, that of technical rationality) can blind us to values associated with double-loop learning and the learning organization, organization adaptability, workforce creativity and development, humanizing the workplace, cultural awareness, and strategy making."

A BusinessWeek article says that James McNerney's introduction of Six Sigma at 3M had the effect of stifling creativity and reports its removal from the research function. It cites two Wharton School professors who say that Six Sigma leads to incremental innovation at the expense of blue skies research. This phenomenon is further explored in the book, Going Lean, which describes a related approach known as lean dynamics and provides data to show that Ford's "6 Sigma" program did little to change its fortunes.

Lack of proof of evidence of its success: In articles and especially on Internet sites and in text books "claims" are made about the huge successes and millions of dollars that Six Sigma has saved. Six Sigma seems to be a "silver bullet" method. But, there seems—somehow ironic—no trustworthy evidence for this in some cases.

Probably more to the Six Sigma literature than concepts relates to the evidence for Six Sigma's success. So far, documented case studies using the Six Sigma methods are presented as the strongest evidence for its success. However, looking at these documented cases, and apart from a few that are detailed from the experience of leading organizations like GE and Motorola, most cases are not documented in a systemic or academic manner. In fact, the majority are case studies illustrated on websites, and are, at best, sketchy. They provide no mention of any specific Six Sigma methods that were used to resolve the problems. It has been argued that by relying on the Six Sigma criteria, management is lulled into the idea that something is being done about quality, whereas any resulting improvement is accidental (Latzko 1995). Thus, when looking at the evidence put forward for Six Sigma success, mostly by consultants and people with vested interests, the question that begs to be asked is; are we making a true improvement with Six Sigma methods or just getting skilled at telling stories? Everyone seems to believe that we are making true improvements, but there is some way to go to document these empirically and clarify the causal relations.

Based on arbitrary standards while 3.4 defects per million opportunities might work well for certain products/processes, it might not operate optimally or cost effectively for others. A pacemaker process might need higher standards, for example, whereas a direct mail advertising campaign might need lower standards. The basis and justification for choosing six (as opposed to five or seven, for example) as the number of standard deviations, together with the 1.5 sigma shift is not clearly explained. In addition, the Six Sigma model assumes that the process data always conform to the normal distribution. The calculation of defect rates for situations where the normal distribution model does not apply is not properly addressed in the current Six Sigma literature. This specially counts for reliability related defects and other not time invariant problems. The IEC, ARP, EN-ISO, DIN and other (inter)national standardization organizations have not created standards for the Six Sigma process. This might be the reason that it became a dominant domain of consultants

Criticism of the 1.5 sigma shift: The statistician Donald J. Wheeler has dismissed the 1.5 sigma shift as "goofy" because of its arbitrary nature. Its universal applicability is seen as doubtful.

The 1.5 sigma shift has also become contentious because it results in stated "sigma levels" that reflect short-term rather than long-term performance; a process that has long-term defect levels corresponding to 4.5 sigma performance is, by Six Sigma convention, described as a "six sigma process." The accepted Six Sigma scoring system thus cannot be equated to actual normal distribution probabilities for the stated number of standard deviations, and this has been a key bone of contention about how Six Sigma measures are defined. The fact that it is rarely explained that a "6 sigma" process will have long-term defect rates corresponding to 4.5 sigma performance rather than actual 6 sigma performance has led several commentators to express the opinion that Six Sigma is a confidence trick.

Chapter 24: Design for Six Sigma (DFSS)

Design for Six Sigma (DFSS) is a separate and emerging business-process management methodology related to traditional Six Sigma. While the tools and order used in Six Sigma require a process to be in place and functioning, DFSS has the objective of determining the needs of customers and the business, and driving those needs into the product solution so created. DFSS is relevant to the complex system/product synthesis phase, especially in the context of unprecedented system development. It is process generation in contrast with process improvement.

Six Sigma process, as it is usually practiced, which is focused on evolutionary and continuous improvement manufacturing or service process development, usually occurs after initial system or product design and development have been largely completed. DMAIC Six Sigma as practiced is usually consumed with solving existing manufacturing or service process problems and removal of the defects and variation associated with defects. On the other hand, DFSS (or DMADV) strives to generate a new process where none existed, or where an existing process is deemed to be inadequate and in need of replacement. DFSS aims to create a process with the end in mind of optimally building the efficiencies of Six Sigma methodology into the process before implementation; traditional Six Sigma seeks for continuous improvement after a process already exists.

DFSS as an approach to design

DFSS seeks to avoid manufacturing/service process problems by using advanced Voice of the Customer techniques and proper systems engineering techniques to avoid process problems at the outset (i.e., fire prevention). When combined, these methods obtain the proper needs of the customer, and derive engineering system parameter requirements that increase product and service effectiveness in the eyes of the customer. This yields products and services that provide greater customer satisfaction and increased market share.

These techniques also include tools and processes to predict, model and simulate the product delivery system (the processes/tools, personnel and organization, training, facilities, and logistics to produce the product/service) as well as the analysis of the developing system life cycle itself to ensure customer satisfaction with the proposed system design solution.

In this way, DFSS is closely related to systems engineering, operations research (solving the Knapsack problem), systems architecture and concurrent engineering. DFSS is largely a design activity requiring specialized tools including; quality function deployment (QFD), axiomatic design, TRIZ, Design for X, design of experiments (DOE), Taguchi methods, tolerance design, Robustification and

Response Surface Methodology for a single or multiple response optimization.

While these tools are sometimes used in the classic DMAIC Six Sigma process, they are uniquely used by DFSS to analyze new and unprecedented systems/products.

Arguments over the separation of DFSS from DMAIC/Six Sigma or Lean Six Sigma

Proponents of DMAIC and Lean techniques might claim that DFSS falls under the general rubric of Six Sigma or Lean Six Sigma. It is often seen that the tools used for DFSS techniques vary widely from those used for DMAIC Six Sigma. In particular, DMAIC practitioners often use new or existing mechanical drawings and manufacturing process instructions as the originating information to perform their analysis, while DFSS practitioners often use system simulations and parametric system design/analysis tools to predict both cost and performance of candidate system architectures. While it can be claimed that two processes are similar, in practice the working medium differs enough so that DFSS requires different tool sets in order to perform its system design tasks. DMAIC Six Sigma may still be used during depth-first plunges into the system architecture analysis and for "back end" Six Sigma processes; DFSS provides system design processes used in front-end complex system designs.

Similarities with other methods

Arguments about what makes DFSS different from Six Sigma demonstrate the similarities between DFSS and other established engineering practices such as Probabilistic design and design for quality. In general Six Sigma with its DMAIC roadmap focuses on improvement of an existing process or processes. DFSS focuses on the creation of new value with inputs from customers, suppliers and business needs. While traditional Six Sigma may also use those inputs, the focus is again on improvement and not design of some new product or system. It also shows the engineering background of DFSS. However, like other methods developed in engineering, there is no theoretical reason why DFSS can't be used in areas outside of engineering.

DFSS, applied to Software Engineering

Historically, although the first successful Design for Six Sigma projects in 1989 and 1991 predate establishment of the DMAIC process improvement process, Design for Six Sigma (DFSS) is accepted in part because Six Sigma organisations found that they could not optimise products past three or four Sigma without fundamentally redesigning the product, and because improving a process or product after launch is considered less efficient and effective than designing in quality. 'Six Sigma' levels of performance have to be 'built-in'.

DFSS for Software is essentially a non superficial modification of "classical DFSS" since the character and nature of software is different from other fields of engineering. The methodology describes the detailed process for successfully applying DFSS methods and tools throughout the Software Product Design, covering the overall Software Development life cycle: Requirements, Architecture, Design, Implementation, Integration, Optimization, Verification and Validation (RADIOV). The methodology explains how to build predictive statistical models for software reliability and robustness and shows how simulation and analysis techniques can be combined with structural design and architecture methods to effectively produce software and information systems at Six Sigma levels.

DFSS in Software acts as a glue to blend the classical modelling techniques of software engineering such as OOD or ERD with statistical, predictive models and simulation techniques. The methodology provides Software Engineers with practical tools for measuring and predicting the quality attributes of the software product and also enables them to include software in system reliability models.

Critics

There are no official standards from international bodies that describe the way of working for DFSS. This can however change in the future.

Section 2: Overview of Lean Principles

Chapter 25: Lean and Toyota Production System (TPS)

Lean manufacturing, lean enterprise, or lean production, often simply, "Lean," is a production practice that considers the expenditure of resources for any goal other than the creation of value for the end customer to be wasteful, and thus a target for elimination. Working from the perspective of the customer who consumes a product or service, "value" is defined as any action or process that a customer would be willing to pay for.

Essentially, lean is cantered on preserving value with less work. Lean manufacturing is a management philosophy derived mostly from the Toyota Production System (TPS) (hence the term Toyotism is also prevalent and identified as "Lean" only in the 1990s. TPS is renowned for its focus on reduction of the original Toyota seven wastes to improve overall customer value, but there are varying perspectives on how this is best achieved. The steady growth of Toyota, from a small company to the world's largest automaker, has focused attention on how it has achieved this.

Lean manufacturing is a variation on the theme of efficiency based on optimizing flow; it is a present-day instance of the recurring theme in human history toward increasing efficiency, decreasing waste, and using empirical methods to decide what matters, rather than uncritically accepting pre-existing ideas. As such, it is a chapter in the larger narrative that also includes such ideas as the folk wisdom of thrift, time and motion study, Taylorism, the Efficiency Movement, and Fordism. Lean manufacturing is often seen as a more refined version of earlier efficiency efforts, building upon the work of earlier leaders such as Taylor or Ford, and learning from their mistakes. However, the modern view takes a more holistic approach where the definition of waste is far more generic. Irregular production with ups and downs in production levels would be considered waste. The goal of Lean then becomes the creation and maintenance of a production system which runs repetitively, day after day, week after week in a manner identical to the previous time period.

Lean principles come from the Japanese manufacturing industry. The term was first coined by John Krafcik in a Fall 1988 article, "Triumph of the Lean Production System," published in the Sloan Management Review and based on his master's thesis at the MIT Sloan School of Management.

Krafcik had been a quality engineer in the Toyota-GM NUMMI joint venture in California before coming to MIT for MBA studies. Krafcik's research was continued by the International Motor Vehicle Program (IMVP) at MIT, which produced the international best-seller book co-authored by Jim Womack, Daniel Jones, and Daniel Roos called The Machine That Changed the World. A complete historical account of the IMVP and how the term "lean" was coined is given by Holweg (2007).

For many, Lean is the set of "tools" that assist in the identification and steady elimination of waste (muda). As waste is eliminated quality improves while production time and cost are reduced. Examples of such "tools" are Value Stream Mapping, Five S, Kanban (pull systems), and poka-yoke (error-proofing).

There is a second approach to Lean Manufacturing, which is promoted by Toyota, in which the focus is upon improving the "flow" or smoothness of work, thereby steadily eliminating mura ("unevenness") through the system and not upon 'waste reduction' per se. Techniques to improve flow include production levelling, "pull" production (by means of kanban) and the Heijunka box. This is a fundamentally different approach from most improvement methodologies, which may partially account for its lack of popularity.

The difference between these two approaches is not the goal itself, but rather the prime approach to achieving it. The implementation of smooth flow exposes quality problems that already existed, and thus waste reduction naturally happens as a consequence. The advantage claimed for this approach is that it naturally takes a system-wide perspective, whereas a waste focus sometimes wrongly assumes this perspective.

Both Lean and TPS can be seen as a loosely connected set of potentially competing principles whose goal is cost reduction by the elimination of waste. These principles include; Pull processing,

Perfect first-time quality, Waste minimization, Continuous improvement, Flexibility, Building and maintaining a long term relationship with suppliers, Autonomation, Load levelling and Production flow and Visual control. The disconnected nature of some of these principles perhaps springs from the fact that the TPS has grown pragmatically since 1948 as it responded to the problems it saw within its own production facilities. Thus what one sees today is the result of a 'need' driven learning to improve where each step has built on previous ideas and not something based upon a theoretical framework.

Toyota's view is that the main method of Lean is not the tools, but the reduction of three types of waste: muda ("non-value-adding work"), muri ("overburden"), and mura ("unevenness"), to expose problems systematically and to use the tools where the ideal cannot be achieved. From this perspective, the tools are workarounds adapted to different situations, which explains any apparent incoherence of the principles above.

Also known as the flexible mass production, the TPS has two pillar concepts: Just-in-time (JIT) or "flow", and "autonomation" (smart automation). Adherents of the Toyota approach would say that the smooth flowing delivery of value achieves all the other improvements as side-effects. If production flows perfectly then there is no inventory; if customer valued features are the only ones produced, then product design is simplified and effort is only expended on features the customer values. The other of the two TPS pillars is the very human aspect of autonomation, whereby automation is achieved with a human touch. The "human touch" here meaning to automate so that the machines/systems are designed to aid humans in focusing on what the humans do best. This aims, for example, to give the machines enough intelligence to recognize when they are working abnormally and flag this for human attention. Thus, in this case, humans would not have to monitor normal production and only have to focus on abnormal, or fault, conditions.

Lean implementation is therefore focused on getting the right things to the right place at the right time in the right quantity to achieve perfect work flow, while minimizing waste and being flexible and able to change. These concepts of flexibility and change are principally required to allow production levelling, using tools like SMED, but have their analogues in other processes such as research and development (R&D). The flexibility and ability to change are within bounds and not open-ended and therefore often not expensive capability requirements. More importantly, all of these concepts have to be understood, appreciated, and embraced by the actual employees who build the products and therefore own the processes that deliver the value. The cultural and managerial aspects of Lean are possibly more important than the actual tools or methodologies of production itself. There are many examples of Lean tool implementation without sustained benefit, and these are often blamed on weak understanding of Lean throughout the whole organization.

Lean aims to make the work simple enough to understand, do and manage. To achieve these three goals at once there is a belief held by some that Toyota's mentoring process,(loosely called Senpai and Kohai, which is Japanese for senior and junior), is one of the best ways to foster Lean Thinking up and down the organizational structure. This is the process undertaken by Toyota as it helps its suppliers improve their own production. The closest equivalent to Toyota's mentoring process is the concept of "Lean Sensei," which encourages companies, organizations, and teams to seek outside, third-party experts, who can provide unbiased advice and coaching.

There have been recent attempts to link Lean to Service Management, perhaps one of the most recent and spectacular of which was London Heathrow Airport's Terminal 5. This particular case provides a graphic example of how care should be taken in translating successful practices from one context (production) to another (services), expecting the same results. In this case the public perception is more of a spectacular failure, than a spectacular success, resulting in potentially an unfair tainting of the lean manufacturing philosophies!

Chapter 26: A Brief History of Waste Reduction Thinking

The avoidance and then lateral removal of waste has a long history, and as such this history forms much of the basis of the philosophy now known as "Lean". In fact many of the concepts now seen as key to lean have been discovered and rediscovered over the years by others in their search to reduce waste.

Pre-20th century

The printer Benjamin Franklin contributed greatly to waste reduction thinking. Most of the basic goals of lean manufacturing are common sense, and documented examples can be seen as early as Benjamin Franklin. Poor Richard's Almanac says of wasted time, "He that idly loses 5s. worth of time, loses 5s. and might as prudently throw 5s. into the river." He added that avoiding unnecessary costs could be more profitable than increasing sales: "A penny saved is two pence clear. A pin a-day is a groat a-year. Save and have."

Again Franklin's The Way to Wealth says the following about carrying unnecessary inventory. "You call them goods; but, if you do not take care, they will prove evils to some of you!

You expect they will be sold cheap, and, perhaps, they may be bought for less than they cost; but, if you have no occasion for them, they must be dear to you.

Remember what Poor Richard says, 'Buy what thou hast no need of, and ere long thou shalt sell thy necessaries.' In another place he says, 'Many have been ruined by buying good penny worths'." Henry Ford cited Franklin as a major influence on his own business practices, which included Just-in-time manufacturing.

The concept of waste being built into jobs and then taken for granted was noticed by motion efficiency expert Frank Gilbreth, who saw that masons bent over to pick up bricks from the ground. The bricklayer was therefore lowering and raising his entire upper body to pick up a 2.3 kg (5 lb.) brick, and this inefficiency had been built into the job through long practice. Introduction of a non-stooping scaffold, which delivered the bricks at waist level, allowed masons to work about three times as quickly, and with less effort.

20th century

Frederick Winslow Taylor, the father of scientific management, introduced what are now called standardization and best practice deployment. In his Principles of Scientific Management, (1911), Taylor said: "And whenever a workman proposes an improvement, it should be the policy of the management to make a careful analysis of the new method, and if necessary conduct a series of experiments to determine accurately the relative merit of the new suggestion and of the old standard. And whenever the new method is found to be markedly superior to the old, it should be adopted as the standard for the whole establishment."

Taylor also warned explicitly against cutting piece rates (or, by implication, cutting wages or discharging workers) when efficiency improvements reduce the need for raw labour; "...after a workman has had the price per piece of the work he is doing lowered two or three times as a result of his having worked harder and increased his output, he is likely entirely to lose sight of his employer's side of the case and become imbued with a grim determination to have no more cuts if soldiering [marking time, just doing what he is told] can prevent it."

Chapter 27: Design for Manufacture (DFM)

DFM is also a Ford concept. Ford said in My Life and Work "the same reference describes just in time manufacturing very explicitly"

Entirely useless parts may be a shoe, a dress, a house, a piece of machinery, a railroad, a steamship, an airplane. As we cut out useless parts and simplify necessary ones, we also cut down the cost of making the product, but also it is to be remembered that all the parts are designed so that they can be most easily made.

This standardization of parts was central to Ford's concept of mass production, and the manufacturing "tolerances" or upper and lower dimensional limits that ensured interchangeability of parts became widely applied across manufacturing.

Decades later, the renowned Japanese quality guru, Genichi Taguchi, demonstrated that this "goal post" method of measuring was inadequate. He showed that "loss" in capabilities did not begin only after exceeding these tolerances, but increased as described by the Taguchi Loss Function at any condition exceeding the nominal condition. This became an important part of W. Edwards Deming's quality movement of the 1980s, later helping to develop improved understanding of key areas of focus such as cycle time variation in improving manufacturing quality and efficiencies in aerospace and other industries.

While Ford is renowned for his production line it is often not recognized how much effort he put into removing the fitters' work to make the production line possible. Until Ford, a car's components always had to be fitted or reshaped by a skilled engineer at the point of use, so that they would connect properly. By enforcing very strict specification and quality criteria on component manufacture, he eliminated this work almost entirely, reducing manufacturing effort by between 60-90%. However, Ford's mass production system failed to incorporate the notion of "pull production" and thus often suffered from over-production.

Toyota develops TPS

Toyota's development of ideas that later became Lean may have started at the turn of the 20th century with Sakichi Toyoda, in a textile factory with looms that stopped themselves when a thread broke, this became the seed of autonomation and Jidoka. Toyota's journey with JIT may have started back in 1934 when it moved from textiles to produce its first car. Kiichiro Toyoda, founder of Toyota, directed the engine casting work and discovered many problems in their manufacture. He decided he must stop the repairing of poor quality by intense study of each stage of the process. In 1936, when Toyota won its first truck contract with the Japanese government, his processes hit new problems and he developed the "Kaizen" improvement teams.

Levels of demand in the Post War economy of Japan were low and the focus of mass production on lowest cost per item via economies of scale therefore had little application. Having visited and seen supermarkets in the USA, Taiichi Ohno recognised the scheduling of work should not be driven by sales or production targets but by actual sales. Given the financial situation during this period, over-production had to be avoided and thus the notion of Pull (build to order rather than target driven Push) came to underpin production scheduling.

It was with Taiichi Ohno at Toyota that these themes came together. He built on the already existing internal schools of thought and spread their breadth and use into what has now become the Toyota Production System (TPS). It is principally from the TPS, but now including many other sources, that Lean production is developing. Norman Bodek wrote the following in his foreword to a reprint of Ford's Today and Tomorrow.

"I was first introduced to the concepts of just-in-time (JIT) and the Toyota production system in 1980. Subsequently I had the opportunity to witness its actual application at Toyota on one of our numerous Japanese study missions. There I met Mr. Taiichi Ohno, the system's creator. When bombarded with questions from our group on what inspired his thinking, he just laughed and said he learned it all from Henry Ford's book."

The scale, rigor and continuous learning aspects of TPS have made it a core concept of Lean.

Chapter 28: Types of Waste

While the elimination of waste may seem like a simple and clear subject it is noticeable that waste is often very conservatively identified. This then hugely reduces the potential of such an aim. The elimination of waste is the goal of Lean, and Toyota defined three broad types of waste; muda, muri and mura; it should be noted that for many Lean implementations this list shrinks to the first waste type only with corresponding benefits decrease. To illustrate the state of this thinking Shigeo Shingo observed that only the last turn of a bolt tightens it; the rest is just movement. This ever finer clarification of waste is key to establishing distinctions between value-adding activity, waste and non-value-adding work. Non-value adding work is waste that must be done under the present work conditions. One key is to measure, or estimate, the size of these wastes, to demonstrate the effect of the changes achieved and therefore the movement toward the goal.

The "flow" (or smoothness) based approach aims to achieve JIT, by removing the variation caused by work scheduling and thereby provide a driver, rationale or target and priorities for implementation, using a variety of techniques. The effort to achieve JIT exposes many quality problems that are hidden by buffer stocks; by forcing smooth flow of only value-adding steps, these problems become visible and must be dealt with explicitly.

Muri is all the unreasonable work that management imposes on workers and machines because of poor organization, such as carrying heavy weights, moving things around, dangerous tasks, even working significantly faster than usual. It is pushing a person or a machine beyond its natural limits. This may simply be asking a greater level of performance from a process than it can handle without taking shortcuts and informally modifying decision criteria. Unreasonable work is almost always a cause of multiple variations.

To link these three concepts is simple in TPS and thus Lean. Firstly, muri focuses on the preparation and planning of the process, or what work can be avoided proactively by design.

Next, mura then focuses on how the work design is implemented and the elimination of fluctuation at the scheduling or operations level, such as quality and volume.

Muda is then discovered after the process is in place and is dealt with reactively. It is seen through variation in output. It is the role of management to examine the muda, in the processes and eliminate the deeper causes by considering the connections to the muri and mura of the system. The muda and mura inconsistencies must be fed back to the muri, or planning, stage for the next project.

A typical example of the interplay of these wastes is the corporate behaviour of "making the numbers" as the end of a reporting period approaches. Demand is raised to 'make plan,' increasing (mura), when the "numbers" are low, which causes production to try to squeeze extra capacity from the process, which causes routines and standards to be modified or stretched. This stretch and improvisation leads to muri-style waste, which leads to downtime, mistakes and back flows, and waiting, thus the muda of waiting, correction and movement.

The original seven muda are:
1. Transport (moving products that are not actually required to perform the processing)
2. Inventory (all components, work in process and finished product not being processed)
3. Motion (people or equipment moving or walking more than is required to perform the processing)
4. Waiting (waiting for the next production step)
5. Overproduction (production ahead of demand)
6. Over Processing (resulting from poor tool or product design creating activity)
7. Defects (the effort involved in inspecting for and fixing defects)

Later an eighth waste was defined by Womack et al. (2003); it was described as manufacturing goods or services that do not meet customer demand or specifications. Many others have added the "waste of unused human talent" to the original seven wastes. These wastes were not originally a part of the seven deadly wastes defined by Taiichi Ohno in TPS, but were found to be useful additions in practice.

Chapter 29: Lean Implementation Develops from TPS

The discipline required to implement Lean and the disciplines it seems to require are so often counter-cultural that they have made successful implementation of Lean a major challenge.

Some would say that it was a major challenge in its manufacturing 'heartland' as well. Implementations under the Lean label are numerous and whether they are Lean and whether any success or failure can be laid at Lean's door is often debatable.

Individual examples of success and failure exist in almost all spheres of business and activity and therefore cannot be taken as indications of whether Lean is particularly applicable to a specific sector of activity. It seems clear from the "successes" that no sector is immune from beneficial possibility.

Lean is about more than just cutting costs in the factory. One crucial insight is that most costs are assigned when a product is designed. Often an engineer will specify familiar, safe materials and processes rather than inexpensive, efficient ones. This reduces project risk, that is, the cost to the engineer, while increasing financial risks, and decreasing profits. Good organizations develop and review checklists to review product designs.

Companies must often look beyond the shop-floor to find opportunities for improving overall company cost and performance. At the system engineering level, requirements are reviewed with marketing and customer representatives to eliminate those requirements that are costly. Shared modules may be developed, such as multipurpose power supplies or shared mechanical components or fasteners. Requirements are assigned to the cheapest discipline. For example, adjustments may be moved into software, and measurements away from a mechanical solution to an electronic solution. Another approach is to choose connection or power-transport methods that are cheap or that used standardized components that become available in a competitive market.

In summary, an example of a lean implementation program could be:

With a tools-based approach:
1. Senior management to agree and discuss their lean vision.
2. Management brainstorm to identify project leader and set objectives.
3. Communicate plan and vision to the workforce.
4. Ask for volunteers to form the Lean Implementation team (5-7 works best, all from different departments).
5. Appoint members of the Lean Manufacturing Implementation Team.
6. Train the Implementation Team in the various lean tools - make a point of trying to visit

other non competing businesses that have implemented lean.

7. Select a Pilot Project to implement – 5S is a good place to start.
8. Run the pilot for 2–3 months - evaluate, review and learn from your mistakes.
9. Roll out pilot to other factory areas.
10. Evaluate results, encourage feedback.
11. Stabilize the positive results by teaching supervisors how to train the new standards you've developed with TWI methodology (Training Within Industry).
12. Once you are satisfied that you have a habitual program, consider introducing the next lean tool. Select the one that gives you the biggest return for your business.

With a muri or flow based approach (as used in the TPS with suppliers.

1. Sort out as many of the visible quality problems as you can, as well as downtime and other instability problems, and get the internal scrap acknowledged and its management started.
2. Make the flow of parts through the system or process as continuous as possible using work cells and market locations where necessary and avoiding variations in the operators work cycle.
3. Introduce standard work and stabilize the work pace through the system.
4. Start pulling work through the system, look at the production scheduling and move toward daily orders with kanban cards.

5. Even out the production flow by reducing batch sizes, increase delivery frequency internally and if possible externally, level internal demand.
6. Improve exposed quality issues using the tools
7. Remove some people (or increase quotas) and go through this work again (the Oh No !! moment).

Lean leadership

The role of the leaders within the organization is the fundamental element of sustaining the progress of lean thinking. Experienced kaizen members at Toyota, for example, often bring up the concepts of Senpai, Kohai, and Sensei, because they strongly feel that transferring of Toyota culture down and across Toyota can only happen when more experienced Toyota Sensei continuously coach and guide the less experienced lean champions. Unfortunately, most lean practitioners in North America focus on the tools and methodologies of lean, versus the philosophy and culture of lean.

KPI and Lean

One of the dislocative effects of Lean is in the area of key performance indicators (KPI). The KPIs by which plant/facility are judged will often be driving behaviour, because the KPIs themselves assume a particular approach to the work being done. This can be an issue where, for example a truly Lean, Fixed Repeating Schedule (FRS) and JIT approach is adopted, because these KPIs will no longer reflect performance, as the assumptions on which they are based become invalid. It is a key leadership challenge to manage the impact of this KPI chaos within the organization.

Similarly, commonly used accounting systems developed to support mass production are no longer appropriate for companies pursuing Lean. Lean Accounting provides truly Lean approaches to business management and financial reporting.

After formulating the guiding principles of its lean manufacturing approach in the Toyota Production System (TPS), Toyota formalized in 2001 the basis of its lean management; the key managerial values and attitudes needed to sustain continuous improvement in the long run. These core management principles are articulated around the twin pillars of Continuous Improvement (relentless elimination of waste) and Respect for People (engagement in long term relationships based on continuous improvement and mutual trust).

This formalization stems from problem solving. As Toyota expanded beyond its home base for the past 20 years, it hit the same problems in getting TPS properly applied that other western companies have had in copying TPS. Like any other problem, it has been working on trying a series of countermeasures to solve this particular concern. These countermeasures have focused on culture; how people behave, which is the most difficult challenge of all. Without the proper behavioural principles and values, TPS can be totally misapplied and fail to deliver results. As with TPS, the values had originally been passed down in a master-disciple manner, from boss to subordinate, without any written statement on the way. Just as with TPS, it was internally argued that formalizing the values would stifle them and lead to further misunderstanding. However, as Toyota veterans eventually wrote down the basic principles of TPS, Toyota set to put the Toyota Way into writing to educate new joiners.

Chapter 30: Continuous Improvement

Continuous Improvement breaks down into four basic principles:
1. Challenge
2. Kaizen.
3. Respect
4. Teamwork

1. Challenge

Having a long term vision of the challenges one needs to face to realize one's ambition (what we need to learn rather than what we want to do and then having the spirit to face that challenge). To do so, we have to challenge ourselves every day to see if we are achieving our goals.

2. Kaizen

Good enough never is, no process can ever be thought perfect, so operations must be improved continuously, striving for innovation and evolution. Going to the source to see the facts for oneself and make the right decisions, create consensus, and make sure goals are attained at the best possible speed.

Respect For People is less known outside of Toyota, and essentially involves two defining principles:

3. Respect

Taking every stakeholder's problems seriously, and making every effort to build mutual trust. Taking responsibility for other people reaching their objectives.

4. Teamwork

This is about developing individuals through team problem-solving. The idea is to develop and engage people through their contribution to team performance. Shop floor teams, the whole site as team, and team Toyota at the outset.

Chapter 31: Is Lean Differences from TPS?

Whilst Lean is seen by many as a generalization of the Toyota Production System into other industries and contexts there are some acknowledged differences that seem to have developed in implementation.

Seeking profit is a relentless focus for Toyota exemplified by the profit maximization principle (Price − Cost = Profit) and the need, therefore, to practice systematic cost reduction (through TPS or otherwise) to realize benefit. Lean implementations can tend to de-emphasise this key measure and thus become fixated with the implementation of improvement concepts of "flow" or "pull". However, the emergence of the "value curve analysis" promises to directly tie lean improvements to bottom-line performance measuments.

Tool orientation is a tendency in many programs to elevate mere tools (standardized work, value stream mapping, visual control, etc.) to an unhealthy status beyond their pragmatic intent. The tools are just different ways to work around certain types of problems but they do not solve them for you or always highlight the underlying cause of many types of problems. The tools employed at Toyota are often used to expose particular problems that are then dealt with, as each tool's limitations or blind spots are perhaps better understood. So, for example, Value Stream Mapping focuses upon material and information flow problems (a title built into the Toyota title for this activity) but is not strong on Metrics, Man or Method. Internally they well know the limits of the tool and understood that it was never intended as the best way to see and analyze every waste or every problem related to quality, downtime, personnel development, cross training related issues, capacity bottlenecks, or anything to do with profits, safety, metrics or morale, etc. No one tool can do all of that. For surfacing these issues other tools are much more widely and effectively used.

Management technique rather than change agents has been a principle in Toyota from the early 1950s when they started emphasizing the development of the production manager's and supervisors' skills set in guiding natural work teams and did not rely upon staff-level change agents to drive improvements. This can manifest itself as a "Push" implementation of Lean rather than "Pull" by the team itself. This area of skills development is not that of the change agent specialist, but that of the natural operations work team leader. Although less prestigious than the TPS specialists, development of work team supervisors in Toyota is considered an equally, if not more important, topic merely because there are tens of thousands of these individuals.

Specifically, it is these manufacturing leaders that are the main focus of training efforts in Toyota since they lead the daily work areas, and they directly and dramatically affect quality, cost, productivity, safety, and morale of the team environment. In many companies implementing Lean the reverse set of priorities is true. Emphasis is put on developing the specialist, while the supervisor skill level is expected to somehow develop over time on its own.

Chapter 32: Lean Goals and Strategy

The espoused goals of Lean manufacturing systems differ between various authors. While some maintain an internal focus, e.g. to increase profit for the organization, others claim that improvements should be done for the sake of the customer.

Some commonly mentioned goals are:
1. Improve quality
2. Eliminate waste
3. Reduce time
4. Reduce total cost

1. Improve quality
To stay competitive in today's marketplace, a company must understand its customers' wants and needs and design processes to meet their expectations and requirements.

2. Eliminate waste
Waste is any activity that consumes time, resources, or space but does not add any value to the product or service.

3. Reduce time
Reducing the time it takes to finish an activity from start to finish is one of the most effective ways to eliminate waste and lower costs.

4. Reduce total costs

To minimize cost, a company must produce only to customer demand. Overproduction increases a company's inventory costs because of storage needs.

The strategic elements of Lean can be quite complex, and comprise multiple elements. We have identified four different notions of Lean.
1. Lean as a fixed state or goal (Being Lean)
2. Lean as a continuous change process (Becoming Lean)
3. Lean as a set of tools or methods (Doing Lean/Toolbox Lean)
4. Lean as a philosophy (Lean thinking)

Steps to achieve lean systems

The following steps should be implemented to create the ideal lean manufacturing system:
1. Design a simple manufacturing system
2. Recognize that there is always room for improvement
3. Continuously improve the lean manufacturing system design.

Design a simple manufacturing system

A fundamental principle of lean manufacturing is demand-based flow manufacturing. In this type of production setting, inventory is only pulled through each production centre when it is needed to meet a customer's order. The benefits of this goal include.
1. Decreased cycle time
2. Less inventory

3. Increased productivity
4. Increased capital equipment utilization

There is always room for improvement

The core of lean is founded on the concept of continuous product and process improvement and the elimination of non-value added activities. The Value adding activities are simply only those things the customer is willing to pay for, everything else is waste, and should be eliminated, simplified, reduced, or integrated. Improving the flow of material through new ideal system layouts at the customer's required rate would reduce waste in material movement and inventory.

Continuously improve

A continuous improvement mindset is essential to reach a company's goals. The term "continuous improvement" means incremental improvement of products, processes, or services over time, with the goal of reducing waste to improve workplace functionality, customer service, or product performance.

For improvement to flourish it must be carefully cultivated in a rich soil bed (a receptive organisation), given constant attention (sustained leadership), assured the right amounts of light (training and support) and water (measurement and data) and protected from damaging.

Chapter 33: Conclusion

Like its predecessors, Six Sigma doctrine asserts that:

Continuous efforts to achieve stable and predictable process results (i.e., reduce process variation) are of vital importance to business success.

Manufacturing and business processes have characteristics that can be measured, analyzed, improved and controlled.

Achieving sustained quality improvement requires commitment from the entire organization, particularly from top-level management.

We should also remember that in order for any process capability to accurately be calculated, one must properly define and quantify the process defect, unit and opportunity. Every process should have definitions for defect, unit and opportunity.

You must remember the following characteristics of Lean Six Sigma

1. Start with the Customer

Before you can define your process defects, units and opportunities, you need to understand the needs of your customers. Voice of the Customer (Customer Needs, eSurveys, Focus Groups, Surveys) is the process of gathering customer comments/quotes and translating them into issues and specifications. From these comments, issues and specifications come the customer CTQ (Critical To Quality) – a product or service characteristic that must be met to satisfy a customer specification or requirement.

2. Define your Product/Service Defects

A defect is defined as any part of a product or service that does not meet customer specifications or requirements, or causes customer dissatisfaction, or does not fulfil the functional or physical requirements. It should be noted that the term customer refers to both internal and external customers.

3. Define your Product/Service Units

A unit is something that can be quantified by a customer. It is a measurable and observable output of your business process. It may manifest itself as a physical unit or, if a service, it may have specific start and stop points.

4. Define your Product/Service Opportunities

Simply stated, opportunities are the total number of chances per unit to have a defect. Each opportunity must be independent of other opportunities and, like a unit, must be measurable and observable. The final requirement of an opportunity is that it directly relates to the customer CTQ. The total count of opportunities indicates the complexity of a product or service.

Good Luck!

www.ingramcontent.com/pod-product-compliance
Lightning Source LLC
Chambersburg PA
CBHW071758200526
45167CB00017B/411